The
Community College
and the
Good Society

The
Community College
and the
Good Society

How the Liberal Arts Were Undermined
and What We Can Do to Bring Them Back

Chad Hanson

Transaction Publishers
New Brunswick (U.S.A.) and London (U.K.)

Library of Congress Catalog Number: 2009041754
ISBN: 978-1-4128-1343-3
Printed in the United States of America

Library of Congress Cataloging-in-Publication Data

Hanson, Chad, 1969-
  The community college and the good society : how the liberal arts were undermined and what we can do to bring them back / Chad Hanson.
       p. cm.
  Includes bibliographical references and index.
  ISBN 978-1-4128-1343-3
     1. Community colleges--History. 2. Community colleges--Plan-ning. 3. Educational change. 4. Education, Humanistic. 5. Vocational education. I. Title.

LB2328.H26 2010
378.1'5430973--dc22

                                                    2009041754

Contents

Acknowledgments

Appreciation goes to my wife, Lynn. She does not like it, but she lets me cloister myself in my office while I work on writing books. I am grateful to Laurie Lye and Amy Dyrek. They sought out the references that formed the basis for these chapters. On that note, I would like to recognize the editors of journals where a number of the ideas herein first saw publication: *Thought & Action*, *The Community College Review*, and *The Community College Journal of Research and Practice*. I need to thank my mother Kathy Anderson. When I was young she taught me how to see injustices. I would also like to thank my grandmother, Marilyn Benson. She clipped grocery coupons out of the *Minneapolis Star-Tribune* and mailed them to me in my dorm room so I could eat while I was away at the university.

Introduction:
What are Community Colleges For?

I did not begin teaching in two-year colleges. I am a product of universities, and I began my professional life conducting research at doctoral institutions. Universities are not perfect. They suffer from a range of problems. Research and grant writing were elevated to God-like status years ago, and to this day undergraduates are treated like inconveniences. I made the move to the community college because I studied the history of education as a graduate student, and I knew that two-year schools were designed to offer the freshman and sophomore years of bachelor's degrees—two years of general education classes—taught by faculty devoted to students and the passing on of academic disciplines. I took up teaching in two-year colleges as a way to take refuge in a place where undergraduate teaching and the liberal arts were valued. At least, that was my intent.

I am mid-way through a rewarding two-year school career, but the community college is not the same institution that it was twenty years ago. The institution has been through cultural turmoil, funding calamities, shifts in the curriculum, and a revolution in technology. The overarching mission of community colleges even changed in notable ways. Workforce training and goals related to economic growth displaced a longstanding commitment to the liberal arts and identity development.

The move toward job training drew strength from the belief that Americans are not equally deserving where education is concerned. Despite all of our talk about equality, there is a pervasive commitment to the thought that we are not equal with respect to our abilities or potential. Realists draw attention to the wide range of SAT and ACT scores earned by college applicants. They also point to differences in grade point averages and graduation rates to suggest that students are not similarly prepared for the rigors of academia.

Of course, some students are better than others, but that situation ought to beg a series of questions, such as: What are we to do, given our obvious diversity? What are community colleges for? Are we to use public schools to exacerbate our students' differences? Should we offer honors seminars for high achievers and welding courses for those with less familiarity with academic norms? Or is it the role of colleges to make us more equal by insisting on a common curriculum—one that lifts the educational floor and binds the nation around a shared experience?

Most of us assume that it is appropriate to steer qualified students toward four-year colleges and universities, but there is a coarse underside to that assumption. In the shadow of our belief in meritocracy, there lies the notion that students from poor families and students with low standardized test scores should feel lucky to have a chance at a round of job training.

When two-year colleges shifted their focus away from preparing students for continued studies and the baccalaureate, our education network became strictly hierarchical. Top-ranked schools continue to serve the sons and daughters of the privileged. Those students continue to receive educations in subjects such as music, history, and physics—the finest and highest achievements of humanity. At the same time, lower-middle class students attend two-year schools where they learn a set of skills of temporary use to businesses.

Only a cynic would suggest that science and art are best reserved for those who can afford to earn a bachelor's degree, but that is the position that we take in the community college. If we held similar expectations for the nation's youth we would recognize the unfairness. For example—if we encouraged students to attend high school through to the end of the senior year, but built a track where they could take vocational courses and graduate as sophomores—we would not tolerate the inequality. We insist that adolescents receive educations that are similar if not equal. For young adults, however, we accept that a portion will pursue and receive bachelor's degrees, while others opt for an education of a different type, one in which they forego time-honored academic traditions.

I am not suggesting that public colleges abstain from teaching skills of value to those who plan to fill roles in the business world. The nation depends on workers who possess unique and marketable skills. In the chapters to follow, however, I suggest that courses focused on narrow, job-related topics are best taught in the third and fourth years of the baccalaureate.

At the moment, students at any one of our postsecondary schools can take classes and acquire capabilities of value in the labor force. The difference is that slightly more than half of our students begin their education in four-year schools, committed to providing two years worth of general education prior to immersion in a narrow field. Whereas, for a growing number of community college students, associate degrees are terminal, and as time goes on those degrees contain fewer courses in the arts and sciences.

Thus, our schools are like bricks stacked up to form the layers of a pyramid. The layers or tiers are not equal, and the price of that inequality grows graver with each passing year. The gap between the wealthy and the poor is now wider than at any point in U.S. history. In a real sense, educational differences lead to fiscal inequality. But there is a more insidious form of inequity that stems from the imbalance in our education levels. The cultural rifts between us have deepened. As the nation's two-year colleges shifted to make vocational training a top concern, our postsecondary schools began to reflect the stratified nature of American society, and today the country is divided on lines made up of contrary values. Political tension grows between the lower-middle class and liberally educated cultural elites.

Our postsecondary schools are marked by difference, but widespread prosperity, a willingness to cooperate, and participation in public life are all crucial to the future of the nation. Our differences keep us from joining together to meet mutual challenges, and there are consequences attached to our failure to share a set of common goals. The problems we face in the twenty-first century will not be solved by citizens narrowly trained to fill positions in the private sector. Businesses have been particularly hesitant to search for solutions to the pressing issues of the day—issues such as global poverty, persistent wars, and climate change.

The century ahead will present us with challenges that will take all of the human potential we have to meet successfully. This book begins with an analysis of the processes that turned two-year schools away from human development, and the last three chapters end with a discussion of the means we could use to restore the promise of a liberally educated population.

The Organization of This Book

C. Wright Mills, the eminent sociologist, claimed that changing social institutions are best understood from the standpoints of history and biography. Throughout the chapters that follow, I attempt to understand how the forces of history—social, economic, and cultural—have influenced the biographies of those who take and teach courses in the community college.

The book is divided into three different parts. In Part One, I examine changes that occurred within two-year schools over the course of the past quarter century. In Part Two, I consider the external forces that shaped the nature of the institution, and in the third part I offer a set of alternatives to the current vocational curriculum.

In the first chapter, I discuss the cultural and political forces that created community colleges. I follow the historical sketch with a discussion of recent changes to the schools' mission and purpose. I propose that the changes would have sparked a debate among figures such as Thomas Jefferson and Alexander Hamilton. The shift away from the liberal arts and toward job training took place without opposition, but I suggest that there are reasons to consider the implications of the new vocationalism.

The second chapter is focused on a revolution in organizational norms and values: learning college culture. I examine books and articles that were crucial to the success of the learning college movement. In the analysis, I suggest that learning advocates pursued an agenda that limited the scope and purpose of public colleges to serving economic, as opposed to broader social roles.

Chapter 3 presents of a study of the competency-based approach to curriculum. In the body of the chapter I evaluate a popular piece of competency-based curriculum software: the Worldwide Instructional Design System (WIDS). The analysis of the WIDS system reveals an educational philosophy that matches the tenets of the learning college movement. In the end, I demonstrate how the software promotes a set of practices that result in the deskilling of teaching and an undermining of educational goals.

In Chapter 4 I analyze the relationship between community colleges and the U.S. Department of Education. Specifically, I conduct an analysis of a report titled, "The 21st Century Community College: A Strategic Guide to Maximizing Labor Market Responsiveness." The report's main themes center on the thought that two-year schools must tailor curriculum to suit the objectives of international businesses. I suggest the approach keeps colleges from attending to their social and political functions.

Chapter 5 contains a brief history and an examination of the work accomplished by the American Association of Community Colleges (AACC). Over the course of the chapter I consider the beliefs and values that guide AACC member's actions. I suggest the group serves as an example of what are called intermediary organizations, and I discuss the Association's efforts to promote occupational programs.

In Chapter 6 I question attempts to propagate an international curriculum. A review of the literature on global education in two-

year colleges led me to conclude that the emphasis placed on globalization stresses the needs of businesses and excludes considerations of either student development or the long-term consequence
of international trade. In contrast, I suggest an understanding of
global economics must evolve from an assessment of local issues
and concerns.

Chapter 7 makes the case for the community college baccalaureate. I consider the arguments both in favor of and opposed to
four-year programs, but I stress the importance of egalitarianism.
Drawing on the work of social historian Christopher Lasch, I make
the point that a hierarchical postsecondary network serves to maintain an unequal class structure. During the course of the chapter, I
stress the baccalaureate's contribution to civic life, and I argue that
academically inclined four-year community colleges are crucial to
fostering a public sphere marked by widespread engagement.

In Chapter 8 I discuss the town hall meeting as a teaching
method. I describe a series of steps teachers can take to bring the
spirit and intent of the town hall meeting to the college classroom.
In addition to describing the technique, I offer a theoretical rationale for the approach, and I also present results from an evaluation
survey.

Finally, in the Epilogue I make an overarching bid for change in
community colleges. In my argument, I place the institution in the
broader context of a shifting educational landscape. Historically,
key institutions advanced to elevated levels in the postsecondary
system. Most notably, teacher's colleges and normal schools both
moved away from the British "collegial" format and toward a German model based on research and specialization—they became
universities. The widespread move from college to university left
a gap in our array of institutions, and as a consequence, American
students have few options in the way of public colleges devoted
to the liberal arts, service or character development. I suggest the
community college is poised to fill that gap in the twenty-first
century.

Part One:

Change on Campus

1

Political Culture:
The Quiet Shift toward Job Training

The community college is an American institution. No other nation supports a network of similar schools on such a wide scale. At present, there are 979 two-year colleges in the United States, enrolling 40 percent of first-time undergraduates. The school is significant to the nation for reasons other than its size, however. The community college acts as a cultural barometer. To understand the community college is to understand how we live and who we are as a society. For the careful observer, two-year schools offer a reflection of the way we see ourselves. They provide us with avenues upon which to pursue our private aspirations, but they also serve as a means for the nation to invest in an array institutions that contribute to a way of life that is consistent with our cultural ideals.

Of course, ideals shift from one generation to the next. Social change is inevitable, but in democracies we assume that the nature of change should be decided through the course of vigorous debate. Public colleges bend their practices to match the desires of people touched by their services, and as such they adjust to the times, but the changes unfolding in two-year schools are taking place without the benefit of open dialogue or critical analysis. Over the course of the past two generations, education scholars maintained a moderate level of interest in the changing nature of the two-year school. In the meantime, however, officials from both political parties became resigned to the idea that community colleges function best when they focus on occupational training as opposed to the liberal arts. Likewise, in the colleges themselves, educational objectives were displaced by goals related to labor force development.

The Stage for a Debate

The community college began as part of a plan to break undergraduate degrees in half—the first two years broad and general, the third and fourth years aimed at immersion in the perspective and methods of a discipline (Deiner, 1986). In their early history, two-year colleges expanded with the purpose of serving as vehicles for providing local access to the freshman and sophomore years of bachelor's degrees, but as community colleges evolved their orientation toward the baccalaureate changed. Community colleges developed multi-faceted missions. In addition to university transfer, they added remedial courses, vocational training, and classes of interest to non-degree seeking students (Blocker, Plummer, and Richardson, 1965). Here, in the twenty-first century, the community college remains comprehensive, but priorities shifted. At present, job training overshadows other aspects of the school's mission or purpose (Ayers, 2005).

In the 1930s, the American Association of Community Colleges (AACC) began promoting vocational curricula, and the focus on training held a prominent place on the agenda of administrators and AACC staff through the forties and fifties (Brick, 1963; Labaree, 1997). Then the 1960s ushered in a set of changes. In the sixties and seventies, "individual and community betterment" became a concern for faculty, irrespective and at times in spite of commercial interests (Levin, 2001, p. 170). The sixties and seventies were a period of social unrest and personal introspection. Community colleges reflected broader cultural patterns by stressing education for the sake of equipping students with the ability to address questions of political and economic justice. The attempt to inculcate such skills enjoyed a short lifespan, however. From the 1980s to the present, community colleges pursued the goal of training personnel to specifications set by employers (Levin, 2001).

During the first wave of vocationalism in the 1930s, students were reluctant to participate. Early occupational programs struggled to enroll an adequate number of trainees, but today vocationalism enjoys a level of support unseen in the past (Dougherty, 1994; Roksa, 2006). At present, an increasing number of community college students enroll in short-term certificate programs, and most students pursuing associate degrees choose occupational majors. In other words, "The occupation-oriented student has become the modal student" (Alfonson, Bailey, and Scott, 2005, p. 209).

In a democracy, change in the nature and purpose of public institutions ought to be the subject of community-wide deliberation, but no such debate took place on the topic of the community college. In the past half century, university-based researchers drew attention to the shift toward vocationalism in two-year schools, but their efforts only produced a smattering of articles, and roughly one book per decade (Clark, 1960; Zwerling, 1976; Brint and Karabel, 1989; Dougherty, 1994; Levin, 2001).

The body of work is small but valuable, as it is the only quarter where questions surface with respect to the motives and consequences of the historic change in the mission of the two-year college. Even so, despite a handful of exceptions (McGrath and Spear, 1991) there have been few public discussions on the subject, and few debates within the schools themselves. The move away from the liberal arts and toward job training advanced without a thorough consideration of the implications or alternatives.

The lack of discourse is vexing since a debate about the community college's shifting mission could easily mirror the debates Americans hold on subjects such as taxation, health care, K-12 education, or the environment. Given the number of Americans affected in some way by community colleges, the institution's role ought to be the subject of ongoing dialogue. For example, questions about the purpose of the school, if raised by students, staff or faculty could easily match the questions that the nation's founders addressed when they fought to forge an understanding of the role civic institutions fulfill in a democracy.

Community colleges receive little public attention, but in early U.S. history national leaders held deep discussions on the subject of social institutions and their function. Of those conversations, the most well known is the debate between Alexander Hamilton and Thomas Jefferson. The two statesmen differed when it came to questions about the purpose of public agencies. They also held contrary views on the role that citizens fulfill in a self-governed society, and their thoughts lend themselves to an analysis of the community college, as the schools' purpose is that of making education available to a broad cross-section of the population.

Hamilton and the Hierarchical Society

Hamilton co-authored the *Federalist Papers*. Together with John Jay and James Madison, the three published a series of eighty-five essays in 1787 urging Americans to adopt a constitution designed to create a strong central government. Hamilton is considered the intellectual force at work in the *Papers*, but it is important to note that his views on the nature of society took shape, not in the new American states, but during his childhood in the West Indies (Staloff, 2005). Eighteenth-century colonial societies were stratified, and Hamilton came to see political and economic inequality as a result of natural distinctions between members of differing social classes. He believed a nation's economy served as an arbiter of personal merit and leadership potential. He assumed, in nations where citizens pursue self-interests, superior individuals rise toward positions of power. In Hamilton's words, "All communities divide themselves into the few and the many. The first are the rich and well born, the other the mass of the people" (*Elliot's Debates* Vol. 4., p. 244, quoted in Parrington, 1927, p. 307).

Hamilton traveled in aristocratic circles and harbored ill feelings toward those he thought of as commoners. In particular, he distrusted their judgment. In his mind, most are unfit to perform civic duties, and he fought to reserve political offices for those with financial means. He wrote, "The people are turbulent and changing; they seldom judge or determine right. Give, therefore, to the first class a distinct, permanent share in government" (*Elliot's Debates* Vol. 4., p. 244, quoted in Parrington, 1927, p. 307). Hamilton's prototype society functioned as a competition where individuals pursue profit in unregulated markets. He claimed that competition separated elites from the masses and from their position at the top of the hierarchy, he believed the dominant class would maintain order and stability.

Hamilton conceived public institutions in the same fashion as he conceived the private sector—an arena where self-interests prevail—and Hamilton's views echo through the literature on community colleges. For example, in *The American Community College* (1987) Cohen and Brawer suggest of the nation's network of two-year schools, "It is a system for individuals, and it does what the best educational forms have always done: it helps individuals" (p. 356). Cohen and Brawer conceive community colleges in terms that are individualistic and, like Hamilton, they exhibit distaste for those given to poor performance in the competition that takes place in the U.S. economy. Kelly and Harbison describe Hamilton's perspective as follows:

> Hamilton was the national spokesman for those of wealth and standing—for the rich, the wise and the well born, as he liked to term them. He neither understood nor sympathized with the great mass of people of little or no property. He simply attributed their incapacity to indolence. (1970, p. 177)

In a similar vein, Cohen and Brawer make it plain that community colleges are not obliged to introduce students from the lower classes to the humanities, scholarship, or the life of the mind; and they suggest that two-year schools do not have the capacity to "make learned scholars of television-ridden troglodytes" (1987, p. 356). Contemporary authors commenting on two-year colleges also hold Hamiltonian views similar to those of Cohen and Brawer (Rouche and Jones Eds., 2005). Few give thought to the role of education in transforming television-ridden troglodytes into citizens with the capacity to analyze their interests or take action in the public sphere.

The move toward a vocational curriculum in the community college is consistent with Hamilton's conception of the role civic institutions fulfill in a capitalist nation. He argued that public institutions function best when they serve supporting roles, propping up the interests of businesses. Parrington suggests, "In developing his policies as Secretary of the Treasury, Hamilton applied his favorite principle, that government and property must join in a close working alliance" (1927, p. 308). Workforce development programs in community colleges embody the sort of alliance Hamilton envisioned, as they represent a tax-supported means to subsidize training costs incurred in the private sector.

Hamilton stressed the idea that a country's citizens are not equal with respect to their potential for success. Thus, a hierarchical network of postsecondary schools suits his philosophy: elite liberal arts colleges and universities to groom leaders, low status vocational institutes to supply businesses with competent, submissive employees. The Hamiltonian framework, when applied to education, favors a network of institutions shepherding citizens to "appropriate," though unequal stations in society.

Jefferson and Popular Sovereignty

In contrast to Hamilton, Jefferson harbored a concern over "the disparities that commercial societies encourage" (Parrington, 1927, p. 46). Jefferson regarded civic virtue as a cornerstone of self-governance, and from his standpoint, social and economic equality were preconditions for creating widespread devotion to public participation. Hamilton preferred social relations where the pursuit of self-interest dominated, but Jefferson's plan for the nation hinged on the hope that citizens would temper their self-interests with a commitment to the common good. In the words of Morton Frisch:

> Hamilton was much more attracted by the commercial aspect than the civic-spirited aspect of a regime. But Jefferson believed that a democratic society must have a more

solid base than acquisitiveness. Civil society, he thought, can be healthy only if the pervasive selfish concern for material well-being and the acquisition of wealth be subordinated to civic-spiritedness. (1991, p. 45)

In opposition to the countries of Europe, where the pursuit of self-interest wrought distinct class divisions, Jefferson's plan for the American nation turned on the development of a civic culture strong enough to bend a diverse society toward common purposes. Jefferson knew, however, that a civic culture alone would not suffice as a means of moderating self-interest or encouraging community involvement. He knew if business life evolved in such a way that a class of elites came to predominate, they would control the affairs of state as well as the economy. Political power would be taken from the hands of working people, and democratic ends would be subordinated to the goals of commerce.

In *Thomas Jefferson and the Development of American Public Education,* James Bryant Conant quotes the third president to the effect that the nation would suffer if we failed to take steps to avail ourselves of the talents, "which nature has sown as liberally among the poor as the rich" (1963, p. 43). Jefferson alleged, if the American school system developed in such a way that the children of well-heeled citizens received an education of a different type than those born into families of modest means, the talents of working people would be left uncultivated. Moreover, he believed if a large pool of talent went undeveloped it would leave a well-educated minority in a position to control public affairs, and he believed a permanent class of elites would use government offices to serve their own interests as opposed to those of the nation.

In contrast to European societies, ruled by landowners and industrialists, Jefferson believed, for Americans, "The future would be better to the degree that mastery passed into common hands" (Parrington, 1927, p. 360). For Jefferson, education held the promise of making citizens, even those of humble means, ready to participate in political processes. Although he did not live to see the birth and subsequent growth of two-year colleges, Jefferson's University of Virginia took the nation one step toward establishing a postsecondary network built to serve a wide cross-section of the polity. He believed public education encouraged a broad commitment to the arts and sciences, and from his standpoint, such a commitment held the promise of ensuring intellectual equality, an essential ingredient in his plan to keep the nation from lapsing into a rigid social class system.

Jefferson worked to avoid the formation of a multi-generational class structure in America, and he tried to convince the nation that a hierarchal order would result if educational opportunities were distributed unequally. Over the course of his life, he encouraged his countrymen to devise and fund a school system with the ability to prepare all citizens to conduct themselves with high levels of creativity and competence. According to Conant, "Jefferson justified his proposals by arguing that if they were adopted, the 'worth and genius—from every condition of life,' would be able to 'defeat the competition of wealth and birth'" (1963, p. 159).

The People's College

There is disagreement about the precise intent of those that played key roles in the founding and growth of two-year colleges, but of the figures that did the most to promote the community college as an institution, the historical record suggests that their goals were Jeffersonian. They intended to offer two years worth of general education, to the broadest number of people, and under the best conditions for fostering the goals of the liberal arts.

Near the turn of the last century, University of Chicago president William Rainey Harper became alarmed by the changing skills and interests of university faculty. In the late eighteen hundreds, leaders in American education became enamored with Germany's postsecondary schools, and in the German university faculty worked in specialized fields characterized by technical expertise. As American universities began to devote themselves to research and graduate training, Harper watched undergraduate teaching lose its place at the heart of the baccalaureate enterprise. By 1900, he publicly lamented the situation that freshman found when they left high schools to enter universities. In an address to the National Education Association, Harper noted of such students, "Not infrequently the instructors under whom they are placed...are inferior to those with whom they have been associated," in public high schools or private academies (1968, p. 55).

For Harper, a division seemed necessary within the four-year curriculum. In order to make the most of his faculty's abilities, he divided the undergraduate program at the University of Chicago into junior and senior colleges. Within the Junior College, expert teachers provided a general education in science and the humanities. After completion of two years of study in the liberal arts, students were eligible for a new credential called an associate degree. He chose the term "associate," because the degree's value was to be realized when it was associated with further study in a discipline. Shortly after Harper's decision to form a junior college within the university, he worked to help Joliet Junior College open its doors as the nation's first public two-year institution.

Meanwhile, on the west coast, two university officials were struggling with the same issue Harper addressed in Chicago. The two figures were David Starr Jordan at Stanford and Alexis Lange at the University of California. Both men shared Harper's concern that general education faltered when American colleges committed themselves to the example set by German universities. At a time when the faculty at Stanford found themselves striving to match their European counterparts in the areas of research and development, Jordan made the following statement:

> There is no worse teaching done under the sun than in the lower classes of some of our most famous colleges. Cheap tutors, unpracticed and unpaid boys are set to lecture to classes far beyond their power to interest. We are saving our money for original research, careless of the fact that we fail to give the elementary training which makes research possible. (1910, p. 441)

Like Harper in Chicago, Jordan became an advocate of community or junior colleges. He argued for a statewide system of two-year schools, the defining feature of which was a faculty committed to teaching excellence. Jordan assumed such institutions could produce graduates with the broad, interdisciplinary background necessary to the process of forming a sound foundation, on which universities would layer specialties.

In the same period, Jordan's colleague Lange also began to suspect that the American imitation of the German system created shortcomings in the area of undergraduate education. In Lange's papers, held at the Bancroft Library on the Berkeley campus, he explains, "Our imitation of Germany has not come far enough" (Gallagher, 1994, p. 10). Specifically, he pointed out that U.S. states failed to create an institution comparable to that of the German gymnasium. As opposed to the university, "In the gymnasium it is the most experienced and most successful teachers that have charge of the work that corresponds to that of the freshman and sophomore years" (Gallagher, 1994, p. 10). Lange successfully urged legislators in California to create the first statewide system of public two-year colleges. From his point of view, the purpose of the institution was to send first-rate educators out to where they could teach courses consistent with the freshman and sophomore years of the baccalaureate, to students from every walk of life and in locations of all kinds.

Historians have been critical of Harper, Lange, and Jordan, on the basis that their efforts to create a network of junior colleges were motivated in part by the thought that two-year schools held the potential to serve as gatekeepers for universities; a means to weed out students ill prepared for upper-division courses (Brint and Karabel, 1989). The criticism is based primarily on the words of Harper. One of his arguments in support of the new institution put him in the position of assuming, with the growth and expansion of two-year schools, "Many students will find it convenient to give up college work at the end of the sophomore year" (Harper, 1968, p. 49).

A century of evidence suggests that Harper read the state of affairs correctly. Fewer students transfer from two- to four-year schools than either he or his counterparts in California imagined. Even so, at the time, the intent of the public two-year college was to provide an increased number of students with instruction on par with their peers in more exclusive institutions. Under the terms outlined by Harper, Lange, and Jordan, if students chose to end their education after the sophomore year, they did so after receiving a general education of equal or better quality than one finds at the nation's most prestigious universities. In contrast, contemporary community college students receive an education that is not only shorter than their peers, but also of a different type (Alfonso, Bailey, and Scott, 2005).

Four-year college students find themselves immersed in art, math, science, music, history, and literature—pursuits that engage us over the span of our lives and in every setting where we find ourselves. Meanwhile, their community college counterparts enroll in a course of study increasingly limited to learning a set of skills with short-term utility, so they can fill ephemeral roles in the rapidly changing labor force.

The Hamiltonian Turn

In the words of Parrington, Jefferson "could not think in terms of the economic man, nor simplify human beings to a labor commodity" (1927, p. 354). In contrast, Hamilton understood the role of public agencies in the terms of economics, and in the past quarter century, community colleges quietly transformed themselves into Hamiltonian institutions. Two decades after the first two-year school opened its doors, community college leaders began turning their backs on the goals and aspirations of the figures that spurred the growth of the movement. Those in positions to influence community colleges began moving the institution away from the goal of providing a liberal arts education to the broadest number of people; instead, they turned the schools toward goals they perceived to be consistent with the financial interests of students and the short-term training needs of businesses.

In a rush to establish themselves as job-training sites, staff and faculty began to think of students as labor commodities. Despite colloquial titles such as "democracy's college" or "the people's college," if current organizational trends continue, historians will be left to discuss the community college solely in terms of its contribution to labor force development (Deikhoff, 1950).

The trend might have appealed to Alexander Hamilton. Within his framework of understanding, public agencies serve fiscal purposes. Nonmaterial goals are overlooked, even though intellectual, aesthetic, and spiritual objectives have also been central to the American civic enterprise (Shapiro, 2005). With respect to Hamilton's views, historian James MacGregor Burns suggests, "Hamilton had worked out everything except what ultimately a nation—even an economically well developed nation—was for" (MacGregor 1965, p. 256). Likewise, we rarely raise questions about the role of the community college in society. We talk about contributing to the economy, but students do not live in the economy, they live in families and neighborhoods. Everyone agrees that students should enter meaningful careers, but we have yet to hold a conversation about how community colleges add to the social or cultural life of the nation. We have yet to ask how two-year schools contribute to what could be called a good society.

When workforce development becomes the purpose of education, students are thought of as a means to reach the business and financial goals of others. They are no longer conceived as ends themselves. By contrast, "A good society is one in which people treat one another as ends in themselves and not merely as instruments" (Etzioni, 2001, p. 2). A community college structured on the lines that Jefferson imagined would approach students as unique threads in our cultural fabric.

In his efforts as Secretary of the Treasury, Hamilton sought to conserve the hierarchy characteristic of the European continent by limiting power and influence to moneyed interests in the upper class. As community colleges moved away from a curriculum centered on liberal learning and toward a focus on training in technical areas, Hamilton's goal of maintaining a culture marked by separate and unequal social spheres became secured (Bishop and Cushing, 2008).

Within the current network of postsecondary schools, institutional goals are diverse. Colleges up and down the ladder of prestige prepare students for unequal positions in society, and even though America's prominence in the world economy serves as a testimony to our ability to place employees at each rank in our business organizations, that ability comes at a high price. Of all the democratic nations on Earth the United States ranks 138th with respect to voter turnout (Lopez Pintor, Gratschew, and Sullivan, 2007). American citizens are well trained when it comes to private sector standards, but with respect to the public sphere we lack the skill and confidence that are required to participate.

A call to revive Jefferson's ideals may seem out of step with current priorities in the community college, but Robert Bellah and associates assure us that education for citizenship is more than a quaint holdover from the nineteenth century. Rather, "It is an essential task for free societies" (Bellah et al., 1997, p. 177). Jefferson railed against the Federalists' assumption that the affairs of the republic are best conducted by elites. He fought to avoid a future where knowledge and power are held in a small number of hands, and despite changes to the schools' mission and curriculum, the community college still holds the key to fulfilling Jefferson's dream of a nation governed by its citizens.

In the contemporary two-year school, there are few conversations about preparing students for roles as leaders or activists, however. Commencement speakers fill their remarks with platitudes about the responsibilities that well-rounded graduates have when it comes to serving their communities, but in the two or more years prior to graduation, most students simply hear messages about the financial advantage of schooling. In the chapter that follows I take a closer look at the process two-year schools went through as they changed their focus from general education to career-specific programs.

2

Organizational Beliefs and Values: The Learning College Movement

At the end of the twentieth century the community college underwent a revolution. The revolution was cultural and linguistic in nature and it was staged in the name of "learning." Personnel in colleges caught in the throws of the revolution altered their beliefs and practices to match an agenda put forth in the literature of the learning college movement. The transformation began in the middle 1990s, and by any measure the initiative succeeded.

Today, more than one decade from its inception, the tenets of the learning college movement are widely accepted. Faculty, staff, and administrators in two-year colleges quickly adopted the language found in learning college texts, and here in the new century the terms and conditions outlined by learning advocates are engrained in the discourse of two-year colleges. The shift was dramatic enough to prompt William Flynn to note, "Whether the topic is the Learning Revolution, a Learning College for the 21st Century, the Learning Organization, or the growth of franchised learning centers throughout the country, we are in the grip of learning-mania" (1999, p. 8).

Never before has learning been a more central focus in two-year colleges. Yet, the heightened focus on learning has channeled the efforts of educators toward purposes that are limited in scope. The focus on learning, in lieu of education, limits the approach of staff and faculty to merely encouraging cognitive, as opposed to social, moral, or aesthetic development (Pascarella and Terenzini, 2005).

Today the goal of producing learning is seen as customary, but learning and education are not one and the same. Learning is private and psychological, whereas education is both social and public. It is possible that learning may be produced by a variety of means. Learning can even take place anytime or anywhere (O'Banion, 1997), but education is a social institution, and the process of becoming an educated person is complex and multi-faceted.

The Russian psychologist Pavlov demonstrated that dogs are capable of learning—so are ducks and mice and barnyard animals (Ciccarelli and Meyer, 2005). Learning is easy to produce and equally simple to measure, however, neither of those can be said of education. Education is a complicated institution, but well-educated citizens are crucial to maintaining the health and sovereignty of free and self-governing nations (Barber, 1992). At best, cognitive development can only be a partial goal for public colleges. Their primary objectives must be social and cultural in character. Post-secondary schools bear the responsibility of "providing the next generation with the capacities, beliefs, and commitments necessary to ensure society's goals" (Shapiro, 2005, p. 37).

It is fair to say that the learning revolution emerged, took hold, and blossomed uncontested. There are few debates about the nature of the revolution in the literature of two-year schools, and few discussions of the matter among staff or faculty (Hanson, 1998, 2003). Community college personnel have placed a longstanding emphasis on student welfare, and, as such, there was little or no resistance to the move toward a language and paradigm alleged to be "learner-centered" (Barr and Tagg, 1995).

In practice, however, there are heavy consequences attached to the process of focusing institutional attention on learning as opposed to education. The revolution has meant more than a mere adjustment to the way two-year college personnel write and speak. In short, the shift had the effect of moving the mission and purpose of community colleges away from public service and toward private sector interests. Levin explains:

With the concept of a learning college emerging as a beacon of change, the purpose of the institution decidedly moved from individual and community betterment to economic ends: development sites for workforce preparation. (2001, p. 170)

In the learning college literature, the aim is to shift the purpose of two-year schools away from objectives that are public and social, and toward goals that are private and psychological—although, the shift is discussed with no mention of the costs or alternatives. The change is described as inevitable, but as Tierney correctly suggests, "A concern with institutional purpose is essentially a moral question that demands a wider range of political and theoretical consideration" (1991, p. 35). Learning college authors make use of terms that sound beneficent; terms like learning, efficiency, and productivity, for example. But a close reading of the texts associated with the movement reveals a pattern of dialogue with dubious implications.

A Sample of the Learning College Literature

In my analysis, I draw from six texts essential to the success of the learning revolution. Robert Barr and John Tagg's 1995 article "From Teaching to Learning" laid the rhetorical foundation for the initiative, and in the words of *Change* editor Ted Marchese, "No recent article in *Change* has attracted the attention of…'From Teaching to Learning: A New Paradigm for Undergraduate Education' which has been reproduced for countless conferences and faculty meetings" (Marchese, 1997, p. 4). The *Change* article was written for a general audience, but at the time the piece was published Barr and Tagg were both two-year college practitioners. Barr was director of institutional research and Tagg was associate professor of English at Palomar College.

In the same month that Barr and Tagg's work appeared in *Change*, George Boggs, then president of Palomar, published "The Learning Paradigm" in the *Community College Journal* (1995). Conceptually, Bogg's work mirrors that of Barr and Tagg, but his 1995 article tailors the learning rhetoric to the mission of two-year colleges.

William Flynn, Dean of Community Learning Resources at Palomar, published "Rethinking Teaching and Learning," four years later (1999). Flynn's position matches that of Barr, Tagg, and Boggs. His work is a restatement of the arguments outlined by Palomar College staff in the 1990s; however, I include the text here because it represents an effort to carry the movement into the twenty-first century.

In addition to the work of Palomar personnel, I sample three texts by Terry O'Banion, one time director of the League for Innovation in the Community College, an organization with the expressed purpose of promoting the learning college agenda. O'Banion is the most prolific author in the learning literature. In this chapter, I consider three of his 1997 publications. The first was written for an audience of college trustees. "The Learning Revolution: A Guide for Community College Trustees," (1997a) appeared as a special issue of *Trustee Quarterly*. I also sample from O'Banion's book, *A Learning College for the 21st Century* (1997b) and from a monograph published with the support of the Peoplesoft Corporation, *Creating More Learning-Centered Community Colleges* (1997c).

These six references are a sample of the books and articles calling for fundamental change in the mission of the two-year school. I took the sample purposefully, with the intent to capture the character of the learning college movement. Although other texts are available, the six samples I consider represent a cross-section of the widely read and broadly referenced works in the literature.

The analysis is presented in two sections. In the first, I examine the rhetorical strategy found in the texts. Throughout the body of work, learning college authors make "proposal" arguments; they ask their readers to "act in a certain way, to do something" (Ramage and Bean, 1989, p. 270). As a point of fact, they ask nothing less of their audience than to "overhaul the traditional architecture of education" (O'Banion, 1997c:11). In the opening section of the analysis I document the techniques learning college authors use to move readers toward enacting change.

In the second section, I consider the impact of the revolution. I give attention to the shift from education to learning in the discourse of the movement, and I also discuss the implications of faculty bending their conception of two-year schools away from that of a public institution and toward that of a business providing services to corporations. In the end, I underscore the consequence of college staff conceiving students as products.

Hostility toward Academic Norms, Roles, and Values

In the 1990s, learning college authors faced a tough task in convincing two-year college personnel that a revolution was necessary. Then, as now, both community college professionals and citizens at large were satisfied with the character and performance of public colleges. In a 2004 article for *The Chronicle of Higher Education*, Jeffrey Selingo described the results of an annual survey designed to measure American attitudes toward postsecondary schools. In 2004, the survey was administered to 1,000 randomly selected men and women aged 25 to 65 and their views are summarized as follows:

> The public's trust in colleges stands near the top among all kinds of institutions, right along with its faith in the U.S. military and in churches and religious organizations. Nearly 93 percent of the respondents agreed that higher education institutions are one of the most valuable resources in the United States. (Selingo, 2004, p. 1)

Public satisfaction with the community college has always been high (Adelman, 1992) and in an environment where people are satisfied, "proposers of change face an extraordinary burden of proof. Specifically, they have to prove that something needs fixing" (Ramage and Bean, 1989, p. 272). For supporters of the learning college movement that meant strong measures were needed.

When the public or a given readership is satisfied with a state of affairs, rhetoricians pushing for change normally accept that "you can't argue what we have is bad," and they hold to a line of reason that suggests, "what we could have is better" (Ramage and Bean, 1989, p. 272). But learning activists pursued a different strategy. They set out to disparage traditional academic culture and institutions committed to the liberal arts, even in spite of their widespread esteem. They began publishing books and articles designed to convince faculty and staff working in two-year schools that the historic norms and values of higher education were detrimental to the health and success of community colleges. Each author sampled here makes an effort to suggest that the goals and objectives of two-year schools are not consistent with those of the academy.

Of the authors sampled here, O'Banion's work is the most hostile toward the institution of education. In his 1997 piece for *Trustee Quarterly,* he quotes Lewis Perelman to the effect that, "The principal barrier to economic progress today is a mind-set that seeks to perfect education when it needs only to be abandoned" (Perelman, 1992, p. 24). In addition, he borrows the language of George Leonard who paraphrases President Ronald Reagan in the context of education (O'Banion, 1997a). The Leonard quote appearing in the O'Banion text reads as follows, "The time has come to recognize that school is not the solution. It is the problem" (Leonard, 1992, p. 26). O'Banion's attempt to clear the way for an alternative to the liberal arts are the boldest in the learning literature, but each author sampled here makes a similar attempt to signal the danger involved in upholding academic traditions.

Barr and Tagg, Boggs, and O'Banion all rely on the work of the Wingspread Group on Higher Education, funded by the Johnson Foundation, to make their case against the academy. Boggs and O'Banion even quote the same passage from a 1993 Wingspread report, titled *An American Imperative: Higher Expectations for Higher Education.* The authors of the report explain:

> A disturbing and dangerous mismatch exists between what American society needs of higher education and what it is receiving. Nowhere is the mismatch more dangerous than in the quality of undergraduate education provided on many campuses. (1993, p. 1)

The situation sounds dire, and learning college activists use the disquieting language of the Wingspread publication to persuade readers that change is needed, but the authors sampled here are focused in the way they excerpt from the Wingspread document.

They use the report to sound an alarm, but they steer a wide path around its conclusions. The Wingspread group offers the following as a solution to the problem they present in *An American Imperative*:

> Every student needs the knowledge and understanding that can come only from the rigors of a liberal education. Such an education lies at the heart of developing both social and personal values. If the center of American Society is to hold, a liberal education must be central to the undergraduate experience of all students. (1993, p. 9)

Learning advocates have made routine declarations along the lines that the liberal arts curriculum is, "just a bunch of courses. It doesn't mean a thing" (Willimon and Naylor, 1995, p. 57). Barr and Tagg's, Boggs's, and O'Banion's appropriation of the Wingspread report's opening sentiments and disregard for its conclusions

Table 2.1
Discursive Practices that Signify Hostility toward Academic Norms and Values

Authors / Dates of Publications	Selected Excerpts
O'Banion (1997a)	Creating a learning centered institution means tossing hundreds of stones into the pond, dumping boulders into the pond, and perhaps even filling in the pond and digging a new one. (12)
Boggs (1995)	The time has come for us to change the way we define the mission of the community college. The paradigm that has guided our institutions from their inception in the early 1900s no longer fits as we approach a new century. (5)
Flynn (1999)	We are trapped inside a house of our own creation, prisoners of a system, structure, and history. (10) After centuries of respect for the academy and the professorate, the focus is now on the learner. (8)
Barr and Tagg (1995)	In the learning paradigm, learning environments and activities are learner-centered and learner-controlled. They may even be "teacherless." (17)
O'Banion (1997b)	It is the business leaders of this country who will confront the academy and prevail. (39)

must be seen as disingenuous, and their selective use of the report points toward a tendency for learning college authors to place the goal of advancing their cause above other considerations. Thus, it is important to reflect on the motivation for the extraordinary steps taken to convince readers that the liberal arts are worthy of contempt.

In the context of British higher education, Barnett has argued that similar calls for reform in the UK were motivated by a growing number of adherents to a culture of science and technology. Barnett claims that scientists define education in different terms than those in the arts and humanities, and in his words, "there was an underlying gulf in the conceptions of what higher education stood for" (1990, p. 106). According to Barnett, scientists see through a lens of measurement and quantification, while those in the humanities are likely to see the college experience as a meaningful part of a student's ongoing development, difficult to assess except in narrative or qualitative terms.

Similarly, in the United States, John Bean suggests that calls for reform have been driven by a growing culture of masculinity that values efficiency and productivity over what are perceived to be feminine concerns: morality, scholarship, and community (Bean, 1998). But Bean offers the most compelling explanation of the underlying force that propels learning college authors when he points out with regard to the terms they use, "it is the language of counting, accountants, accountability and, to a greater or lesser extent, it is how we imagine our enterprise" (Bean, 1998, p. 497). The learning college movement is driven by the language of business.

Learning college activists have worked to disparage the word "education," traditionally associated with broad public purpose, in order to help elevate the term "learning" to prominence. Learning is easier to conceive in private and individualistic terms, and the word "learning" is also more palatable to educators than the term "training," a favorite in the private sector. The discourse of the learning college movement is designed to sweep the language of public purpose aside in order to make room for the instatement of terms that narrow institutional focus down to the level of learning outcomes valuable to businesses. Learning college authors take deliberate steps to disparage the traditions of the academy because they are at odds with the flat assertion that, "The learner's purpose is to please employers" (Ayers, 2005, p. 542).

The Consequence of Shifting from Education to Learning

An examination of O'Banion's "six key principles" for learning colleges creates an understanding of the extent to which an author will go to replace the idea of public education with terms that are individualistic (O'Banion, 1997c, p. 15). O'Banion's principles consist of six sentences, and within those sentences the terms learn, learner, or learning appear seventeen different times (see Table 2.2). Within the learning college movement, the terms student, teacher, and education are conspicuous by their absence.

From a linguistic standpoint, the word "student" implies "teacher," and in a learning college, teachers are thought of as barriers to

Table 2.2
Learning College Principles

- The *learning* college creates substantive change in individual *learners*.

- The *learning* college engages *learners* in the *learning* process as full partners, assuming primary responsibility for their own choices.

- The *learning* college creates and offers as many options for *learning* as possible.

- The *learning* college assists *learners* to form and participate in collaborative *learning* activities.

- The *learning* college defines the roles of its *learning* facilitators by the needs of the *learners*.

- The *learning* college and its *learning* facilitators succeed only when improved and expanded *learning* can be documented for its *learners*.

Source: O'Banion, 1997c, p. 15.
Note: italics added.

the creation of "environments and activities" that are potentially "teacherless" (Barr and Tagg, 1995, p. 17). The terms "student" and "teacher" also carry other connotations. The words student and teacher suggest an institution—education—and for learning advocates, traditional liberal arts education with a broad public purpose is anathema to the goal of turning community colleges into learning colleges with the expressed purpose of subsidizing corporate training costs. When community colleges become learning colleges, two-year school practitioners begin to assume that the sole objective of their work is to move students toward meeting standards set by employers. According to Ayers, in the minds of learning activists, "needs tangential to this purpose are irrelevant" (2005, p. 542). Furthermore, as community colleges make themselves over into learning colleges, organizational structures start to match those found in for-profit industries. Levin offers the following prediction for the American two-year school if the learning college movement goes unchecked:

> ...community colleges will function more on a model compatible with business norms: a fluid organization, with little reverence for academic traditions, little evidence of a dominant professional class of faculty and more evidence of a professional managerial class, more emphasis on technology and less on full-time labor. (2000, p. 21)

The learning movement is an attempt to transform community colleges into business-like employee training camps for entities in the economy. Yet, in the transition from community college to learning college, "There is little or no consideration of the possibility that on occasion the interests of the community and that of employers might actually be opposed" (Dougherty and Bakia, 2000, p. 221). The character of the movement is captured by a slogan made popular in the decade after World War Two, "What is good for General Motors is good for America." In the articles by both Boggs and Barr and Tagg, the General Motors Corporation is held up as an example for colleges to follow. Although the example seems ironic in the current era of flagging car sales and corporate bail-out packages, the GM model is used to encourage faculty to imagine community colleges as organizations where the bottom line is all that matters—training employees for service to multinational companies.

Comparing two-year colleges to auto manufacturers has the effect of minimizing the importance of educational processes, and the comparison also has the effect of heightening the conception of students as products. For example, Boggs uses the GM analogy to create a sense that there would be grave consequences, "if General Motors were to see its business as defined by the assembly line rather than the production of automobiles" (1995, p. 6).

Barr and Tagg continue the metaphor by mocking colleges that care about the nature and the quality of the process students move through on their way to graduation. They claim an overt focus on the process by which students are educated, "is like saying that General Motors' business is to operate assembly lines" (1995, p. 9). In addition, they go on to harden their preference for products

Table 2.3
Discursive Practices that Define Education as a Product

Authors / Dates of Publications	Selected Excerpts
Barr and Tagg (1995)	In the learning paradigm a primary drive is to produce learning outcomes more efficiently. (11)
Boggs (1995)	The mission should be student learning, and we should measure our effectiveness based upon student learning outcomes. (6)
O'Banion (1997c)	"What does this learner know?" and "What can this learner do?" are questions that provide the framework of documenting outcomes, both for the learner and learning facilitators. (20)
Flynn (1999)	Curriculum should be designed around the critical learning outcomes necessary for success in a field. (12) A curriculum built on outcomes gives learners the knowledge, skills, and attitudes that are valued by employers. (13)

over processes by dictating the overall mission of higher education. They write, "Our mission is that of producing *learning* with every student by *whatever* means" (1995, p. 9).

In the automotive industry, lengthy considerations of the manufacturing process are secondary to the assessment of final products—finished cars and trucks. It is fair to assume that automobiles can be manufactured by *whatever* means—the means that are most efficient or the means that contribute the most to quality. Car parts have no preference for one manufacturing process over others, but that is due to the fact that car parts do not own either minds or memories. In contrast, students possess both.

The discourse of production and efficiency is appropriate for manufacturing, but when applied to education the terms lose conceptual purchase. Educational institutions change identities (Chickering, 1972) and the human self or identity is a collection of memories (Mead, 1934; McCall and Simmons, 1966). For graduates, a college is an Alma mater, a set of experiences, and a bundle of recollections that confer social status and order behaviors across the course of entire lives. In the words of Howard Bowen, "the impact of higher education is likely to be determined more by the kind of people college graduates become than by what they know when they leave college" (Bowen, 1977, p. 270). Accordingly, "The proper study of the effects of college…is the study of lives" (Sanford, 1962, p. 809).

Conclusion

Learning colleges discount their commitment to education for the common good and, in the process, they short-change students and society. For example, in the words of the eminent psychologist B.F. Skinner, "Education is what survives when what has been learned has been forgotten" (1964, p. 484). Colleges focused solely on learning outcomes cannot fulfill their social or public obligation, and when colleges focus exclusively on learning they abrogate their responsibility to make prudent long-term investments with public funds.

The authors of the texts I sampled ask two-year school professionals to focus on the short term and the observable, under the assumption that community colleges must alter their curriculum and practices at a pace that matches that of the economy. In fairness, the economy is changing quickly, but the abilities that make a person a successful member of a community have not changed at any point in American history. The thoughts, dispositions, and habits of mind that make someone an educated person and an asset to a community are the same now as they were when Washington crossed the Delaware, and once students find themselves in possession of those traits, they last.

The success of the learning revolution has hinged on the ability of authors to conceal or minimize the importance of proud phrases like "public education for the common good," and with terms like "public" and "education" removed from the discourse, learning activists installed a more individualistic goal for two-year colleges, "learning for the sole purpose of earning" (Levin, 2001, p. xx). At present, it would appear that learning advocates have reached their goal. The rhetoric of learning is so pervasive, many of us "imagine that no other world is possible" (Bean, 1998, p. 496).

On the current state of our imagination, Zemsky, Wegner, and Massey write, "As more people have viewed higher education as offering mainly personal advantages, colleges have virtually given up defining themselves in terms of their contributions to the community, state, or nation" (2005, p. B6). The same authors point out, with respect to the turn away from community and toward the needs of corporations, "When a college or university is wholly dominated by market interest, it sacrifices much of its capacity to serve its public purposes and sometimes even its fundamental mission" (2005, p. B6). Despite the obvious lament of authors Zemsky, Wegner, and Massey, they suggest "there will be no return to a simpler era when market forces played a less dominant role in American higher education" (2005, p. B6) adding and air inevitability to the transformation of our institutions. Yet, as unlikely as change seems in these times, community college professionals would do well to recall a key lesson of history. This is not the first era where market forces and the language of business have come to predominate.

In the words of educational historians Carnoy and Levin, "Just as the period 1880-1929 witnessed the emergence and consolidation of the political power of big business in America," in the four decades that followed, Americans saw, "the decline of corporate power and the success of social movements in winning social reform" (1985, p. 11). Those social reforms included civil rights, women's advocacy, and environmentalism, right up to and including the movement that gave birth to the rapid construction of two-year schools from coast to coast.

In a speech delivered to the American Association of Community Colleges on April 26, 2004, President George W. Bush expressed the view that community colleges operate best when they are, "willing to listen to the needs of those who are looking for workers" (Rouche and Jones, 2005, p. ix). Such sentiments represent a significant shift, as in the past community colleges served the needs of citizens. "Historically, the meaning of *public* education was precisely what it meant to belong to a public: education in the *res publica*—in commonality, in community" (Barber, 1992, p. 14). The needs and interests of American citizens are not identical to those of multinational corporations. Similarly, the abilities essential for participation in the life of our democracy are often different than the skills required to fill a role in the economy. Again, Barber's words are instructive. He writes, "Education in vocationalism, pre-professional training, what were once called the 'servile arts' may be private, but public education is general education for citizenship" (1992, p. 15).

Corporations are not obliged to contribute to the social, cultural, or political life of the nation, but public tax-supported institutions have responsibilities. If college faculty and staff do not take a purposeful set of steps to win back the language of public education for the common good, the movement toward the terms of economic self-interest will continue to prevail. Words make a difference in the way we live and work. Thus, with respect to the American two-year school, I suggest the following: education is the focus, students are citizens not products, and in the spirit of our proud historic mission, the institutions are "community" colleges.

In the chapter that follows, I consider the competency-based approach to curriculum. Community colleges across the country started to focus their efforts on competencies or learning outcomes, beginning in the decade of the 1990s. When two-year schools implemented the model and purchased competency-based curriculum packages, educators began to focus on the measurable outcomes of courses or programs. In the process, teachers began to view their students as products and education as a form of manufacturing.

3

Educational Practices:
Competency-Based Education

The learning college movement brought a focus on the cognitive outcomes of education to a fevered pitch in the decade prior to the turn of the century. The era was also characterized by an emphasis on assessment and accountability. In response to pressures from multiple sources, two-year schools began laying plans to document that students acquire cognitive abilities and career-related skills.

In this chapter, I discuss the practical, on-campus implications of the move toward documenting learning outcomes. I explore the impact of standardized curriculum development software on teaching practices, and I suggest that the work of professional educators is deskilled when colleges demand the use of course planning technology.

The Deskilling of Two-Year College Teaching

Following the publication of Harry Braverman's *Labor and Monopoly Capital*, sociologists began to suggest that the work of teachers could be deskilled in the same fashion as industrial labor. In 1992, Apple and Jungck warned of the consequence when administrators, "borrow the ideology and techniques of industrial management" (p. 24). At the time, they drew attention to the tendency for the curriculum to become, "increasingly planned, systematized, and standardized at a central level, totally focused on competencies," and by the end of the decade American school teachers worked in an environment of standardized lessons and state-wide testing (1992, p. 24). Apple and Jungck's words were prescient, the professions of elementary and secondary teaching have been deskilled or proletarianized, and there are signs the twenty-first century is bringing the same process to community colleges.

On the application of deskilling theory to postsecondary schools, Rhoades suggests, "The recent history of higher education is one of managers initiating the reshaping of colleges' and universities' missions, organization, and instructional programs," and he adds, "deskilling theory's thesis that managers introduce new technologies to increase control over workers makes sense in this context" (1998, p. 182). In this chapter, I argue along with Rhoades that higher education is not immune to the process of deskilling, and I use research by Barnett, Apple and others to explain how the efforts of a growing number of educators is changing as a result of initiatives designed to manage the practice of college teaching. Specifically, I use the case of the Worldwide Instructional Design System (WIDS) to demonstrate how the work of community college teachers is undergoing a deskilling process.

WIDS and Competency-Based Education

In the 1990s, driven by a culture of assessment and accountability, higher education leaders began searching for techniques to document student learning outcomes. Competency-based education, also known as mastery or performance-based education, appealed to managers because the approach requires a practice where teachers make use of curriculum models that document the skills that students develop. The hallmark of competency-based systems is a preoccupation with outcomes, and colleges began to adopt the competency-based approach (hereafter, CBE) under the assumption that the model offers a means to narrow the focus of large, complex institutions down to the level of measurable results. For example, in June of 1992 the Wisconsin Technical College System Foundation joined General Electric Medical Systems in an effort to create a curriculum package that could be used to ensure that college graduates met GE's training specifications. The fruit of their effort was a computer program and support organization called the Wisconsin Instructional Design System, rooted in the competency-based philosophy (WIDS, April 2005).

Ten years after the software's creation, the WIDS client list swelled to include all sixteen schools in the Wisconsin Technical College System, ten Michigan community colleges, and an assortment of two- and four-year schools in eleven other U.S. states. By the spring of 2002, the list of colleges licensed to use the software spread over the border into Canada. Hence, the word Wisconsin was dropped from the title and replaced by, "Worldwide" (WIDS, May 2005).

Competency-based education is often described in terms that sound beneficent. Advocates use terms like "student-centered" and "learner-focused" to describe the approach, although a close reading suggests that in spite of appeals to students and learning, the push toward a competency-based curriculum "is not an educational or professional movement, but a managerial movement" (Bates, 1992, p. 4). Bates explains that competency-based education did not grow out of an ambition to enlighten or enrich the lives of students. Rather, it grew out of a desire to document that colleges produce results consistent with the demands of businesses employing graduates. According to Bates, the purpose of CBE is "increased efficiency and increased articulation between industry and education" (1992, p. 4).

When teachers use WIDS software to create course syllabi or lesson plans they work through a set of steps—each step marked by a question. The first step is to ask "what" students are to learn. The "what" step is followed by the question of "when" students are to meet competencies, and finally faculty members describe "how" students are to demonstrate their skills (WIDS, May 2007). In a WIDS classroom, teachers tell students what to do and successful students comply. At no point do teachers or students stop to ask, "Why?"

Apple predicted a shift away from the "why" question as early as 1986, half a decade before WIDS was introduced to community colleges. In *Teachers and Texts* he wrote, "The more new technology transforms the classroom, the more a technical logic will replace critical political and ethical understanding;" he went on to claim, "the discourse of the classroom will center on technique," and he suggested, "'how to' will replace 'why'" (1986, p. 171). In the case of WIDS, Apple's predictions were right. The missing "why" question is more than a careless omission. Competency-based education is not designed to provide students with a forum in which to wrestle with big questions like, "Who am I? What might I become? What is this world in which I find myself, and how might it be changed for the better?" (Edmundson, 2004, p. 5). The expressed purpose of CBE is to produce a trained and dutiful workforce. Students do not raise questions as part of the curriculum. Thus, with respect to the nature of CBE, Barnett suggests that it is "a conception that sees human beings as mere performers rather than reflective actors. It is a philosophy devoid of enlightened and critical reason" (1994, p. 77). In the WIDS model, there is no room for students to question the tasks they are given.

Corporations may have profit-driven motives for placing rigid demands on employees, despite their personal needs or interests, but those motives are not consistent with the purpose of postsecondary schools. Again, Barnett's words are informative. He writes, "Competencies and outcomes cannot provide guidelines for higher education curriculum. It is the business of higher education to develop critical capacities, which must include the evaluation and possible repudiation of contemporary competencies" (1994, p. 81).

Traditionally, faculty pursued knowledge within disciplines and then they shared that knowledge with students, often through the course of heated debates. As a result, students carried new perspectives and habits of mind into society, but within the WIDS model the traditional process is overturned. In the WIDS system, economic institutions outside the academy determine what knowledge is important. The role of the teacher is reduced to transforming that knowledge into training regimens.

In the arts and sciences, academic freedom and the unfettered pursuit of truth are valued as ideals, but the WIDS model limits the intellectual terrain available to both students and faculty. Students are held to prearranged standards and teachers are beholden to the demands of employers. Since the underlying logic of the WIDS system is that of the marketplace, students are not conceived as adults, citizens, or members of communities. They are merely thought of and described as workers—middle-skilled employees for regional labor markets.

As such, WIDS is characteristic of Taylorist or "scientific" management (Taylor, 1967). Frederick Taylor's time and motion studies served as the basis for an engineering movement that altered the state of the industrial labor force. Under the banners of logic and rationality, scientific management transformed global manufacturing into an entity obsessed with productivity, and the Wisconsin Technical College System Foundation takes steps to maintain the impression that WIDS software is a logical extension of scientific principles.

For example, throughout the WIDS literature there are a number of citations, but the authors cited endorse a diverse set of perspectives. Some of their ideas support a CBE framework, but others lie in conflict with the outspoken intent of WIDS and competency-based education. For example, the WIDS model fits neatly with the performance-based learning approach of Robert Mager, but in contrast, the WIDS model is an affront to the work of the adult learning theorist Malcolm Knowles (Mager, 1975; Knowles, 1973). On the WIDS website, and in WIDS promotional materials, performance-based learning advocates and adult learning scholars are listed side-by-side as authors whose books and articles have informed the development of WIDS, but the work of scholars such as Knowles stand opposed to the basic tenets of competency-based education.

Knowles introduced the concept of andragogy, or student-centeredness, to the postsecondary community, and his work is a challenge to the CBE model where students are conceived as subordinates. The WIDS system is said to be consistent with adult learning principles, but competency-based education is at odds with the body of theory and research that suggests adult students benefit when they are involved in the planning and assessment of their own education.

In spite of claims that WIDS is learner-centered, competency-based models reduce the role of students to merely passing through linear sets of preordained objectives. The nature of the educational process is neglected as teachers focus on the product of their work—student learning outcomes. In short, "This ideology is concerned much more with 'outcomes' than with the character of any pedagogical process. In this pedagogy, to arrive is infinitely better than to travel" (Barnett, 2003, p. 151).

Braverman offers an explanation for the contradictions in WIDS literature. The conflict among authors listed as references belies the fact that the purpose is sales and promotion, as opposed to scholarship. Braverman argued that the intent of scientific management is not the advancement of science. On the contrary, he suggested scientific management "enters the workplace not as the representative of science, but as the representative of management masquerading in the trappings of science" (Braverman, 1974, p. 86). Despite efforts to promote a scholarly image, standardized curriculum software packages like WIDS are best seen, not as a means for improving the art or science of teaching, but as industrial-era management techniques.

The Elements of Deskilling or Proletarianization

With respect to the work of school teachers, Ozga and Lawn suggest deskilling or proletarianization result when an educator is "deprived of the capacity to both initiate and execute work," and they further explain that deskilling entails "the separation of conception from execution, and the breaking down of execution into simple, controllable parts" (Ozga and Lawn, 1988, p. 324). WIDS and CBE are components of a proletarian root system growing in the cultural soil that forms the foundation of community college education. Using Ozga and Lawn's three-part definition, it can be shown that two-year schools have undergone a series of changes consistent with the proletarianization thesis. In colleges where WIDS has been adopted, faculty face all three signs of deskilling.

A Loss of the Capacity to Initiate and Execute Work

When WIDS is licensed for use, the system is ordered and paid for by management. The college-wide adoption of WIDS often gives rise to a dispute over the terms or efficacy of the competency-based approach, but even in schools where the faculty are organized into collective bargaining units, teachers have been unable to stop an institution from moving toward the WIDS model if there is an impetus from administrators or boards of trustees. In fact, few have made efforts to resist.

The lack of opposition is due in part to the fact that "technology is seen as an autonomous process. It is set apart and viewed as if it had a life of its own, independent of social intentions, power, and privilege." (Apple, 1986, p. 151). WIDS software is not neutral, however, and faculty who are made to use it would do well to ask, "Who gains power and who loses it when such presumably neutral technological innovation is introduced?" (Burris and Heydebrand, 1984, p. 202).

In the WIDS model, the work of faculty is no longer conceived as a disciplinary effort to pass on and advance academic fields. Instead, faculty work is considered part of an institutional effort to document student learning outcomes, not a bad goal in itself, but hardly a substitute for the practice of academic freedom within scholarly disciplines. In *On Competence*, Grant offers a summary of the changes that take place when institutions adopt a competency-based curriculum. He writes:

> Course planning is no longer the province of the individual teacher or the teacher's disciplinary guild. The process of curriculum revision and course design in competence-based programs often leads to a coordinated syllabus, sometimes expressed in a condensed form as a "grid" of outcomes and prescribed experiences. In this respect, syllabi in competence programs come to resemble those characteristic of elementary and secondary schools. (1979, p. 14)

Whether or not it is label as such, the competency movement has taken a firm hold in elementary and secondary schools. WIDS merely represents the most recent attempt to move the model up to the postsecondary level, and it is a move that managers are ever more willing to make, as the model is consistent with the assessment and accountability movements shaping the norms and values that give order to life in community colleges.

In fairness, there is no reason why software packages like WIDS should not be available to faculty. But WIDS is not presented as a choice. Teachers are forced to adapt their practices to the WIDS format in schools that purchase a license to use the software, and, on the subject of changing teaching practices to match technological goals, Rhoades suggests:

> Faculty's collective input and control regarding these decisions is in part a proxy of their autonomous control of the curriculum. So, too, is their individual choice about whether to use new instructional technologies. To the extent that managers may direct faculty to utilize such technology in delivering courses, they have reduced faculty's autonomy. (1998, p. 185)

As faculty autonomy is reduced, teachers lose a share of their independence and decision-making power and the loss of the capacity to conduct work on one's own terms is a central feature of deskilling.

The Separation of Conception from Execution

The expressed goal of WIDS products and services is the development of an institutional curriculum that is "systemic, systematic, and consistent" (Soine, 2003, p. 38). In other words, when a college adopts the WIDS model, the curriculum is standardized with the intent that it can be passed from one group of teachers to another.

As a result, the number of faculty that determine the nature of the curriculum is small: those employed full-time when the model is implemented. Subsequent groups of faculty inherit a curriculum established by others.

Furthermore, in the last decade more than half of the newly hired teachers in higher education have been part-time or adjunct (Rice, 2004). In the WIDS system, part-time teachers are asked to use curricula created by full-time employees. Thus, WIDS creates a setting where one group of faculty and staff develop a curriculum that legions of others follow—part-time teachers in particular. According to Rhoades, in such cases, "Instruction is deskilled to consist of simply delivering a course developed by someone else" (1998, p. 201).

The Breaking Down of Execution into Simple Parts

On the measure of reducing complex professional activities to a series of simple parts, there are perhaps no better examples than WIDS and CBE. The WIDS model was designed to limit the work of teachers to a step-by-step set of procedures; faculty fill in the blanks. If a teacher subscribes to the WIDS philosophy and uses the software the way it was meant to be used, every day of the week is prescribed and runs according to a list of competencies, assessments, and objectives. Faculty focus on measurable outcomes, as they should to some degree, but the narrow focus comes at the expense of an emphasis on larger social or educational goals, and according to Apple and Junck, "When complicated jobs are broken down into atomistic elements, the person doing the job loses sight over the whole process and loses control over her or his own labor" (1992, p. 22).

Conclusion

Despite a strong emphasis on accountability in the literature on competency-based education, WIDS software and its accompanying training package have not been evaluated. As of this writing, there has been no systematic attempt to assess the model on the part of the software's creators or any of the colleges that utilize the package. There is no record of faculty, student, or public satisfaction with WIDS, and there is no documentation available to show that implementing WIDS software improves student development or the teaching of academic disciplines (WIDS, May 2007).

In a culture of increased accountability, the lack of scrutiny may come as a surprise, but deskilling theorists have argued that technological systems like WIDS have little to do with assessing or improving professions like college teaching. Instead, they argue that models like WIDS are extensions of management initiatives. WIDS is an attempt to break down, simplify, and manage the work of educators, who have historically conceived themselves as autonomous.

Nevertheless, it is safe to assume that attempts to standardize and oversee the work of faculty will become more common in the future. Pressure to introduce technological management systems into college classrooms will increase, despite evidence suggesting that teachers perform best when they plot their actions according to the needs of students or the demands of their subjects, as opposed to a list of outcomes prescribed by employers.

The learning college movement and the broader culture of accountability and assessment have made it difficult to conceive education as a social institution or as a process that changes lives and personal identities. Within the framework of competency-based education, it is easy to forget that the exercise of creativity, wit and imagination are subjective enterprises that do not lend themselves to assessment in the same sense that technical skills lend themselves to measurement.

The pressure to evaluate is strong, but the force behind the accountability movement is the belief that the American people are dissatisfied with their colleges and that is a questionable notion. Recent surveys suggests there are only two institutions that Americans trust and favor more than higher education—the church and the military (Selingo, 2004). Ironically, the church and the military are two institutions that cannot be accountable to their constituents. For example, churches would fall into disarray if parishioners began demanding assessment reports to document that their prayers had been heard and acted upon. Similarly, for reasons of national security, the armed services must maintain a high level of secrecy with respect to their operations. Neither the church nor the military could ever be accountable to the people that they serve, and yet these institutions are among our most popular and well funded.

Even if there were reasons to believe that the public was dissatisfied with the current state of higher education, there are real questions with regard to whether they would take the time to read and reflect upon formal course or program outcomes statements, and there is further reason to be skeptical about whether the American people would sift through college assessment reports if they were made available. Ongoing surveys by the National Endowment for the Arts make it plain that it is increasingly unlikely for the Americans to read even the most riveting novels or well-crafted poems. There is no reason to think that the public would take time to read assessment reports.

In the months and years ahead, it will be crucial for educators to consider the implications of changing teaching practices to match the goals associated with course management technology, and it will also be vital for faculty to have a role in the discussions that take place around the changing mission of public colleges. Barnett suggests the language of competency-based education, "has to be recognized for what it masks, embedded interests have to be dug out and exposed; otherwise, they will continue to influence and diminish our practices" (1994, p. 55). In a limited sense, the process of deskilling has already infiltrated our institutions. If faculty are to maintain their status as professionals, and if community colleges are to serve a broader purpose than merely providing the private sector with "a free supply of trained subordinates" (Veblen, 1957, p. 144), then competency-based curriculum models like WIDS must be understood for what they are: industrial-era management systems.

The study of the ways in which teaching has been deskilled draws attention to the relationship between schools and the wider society. The work of educators is impacted by the political economy. To a large degree, community colleges have been influenced by external forces. In the section to follow, I consider how two-year schools have been affected by the actions of organizations such as the United State's Department of Education and the American Association of Community Colleges.

Part Two:

External Forces and Their Impact

4

Government Agencies:
The U.S. Department of Education

In the past thirty years, a consensus formed around the thought that two-year schools function best when they offer short-term vocational programs. But in the past, there were disagreements among scholars over the question of why community colleges came to favor job training, and there have also been disagreements over the question of who promoted the agenda.

In this chapter, I discuss a series of rationales that have been used to explain the shift in focus from the liberal arts to occupational training. I begin by describing three explanations for the move. Then I go on to use the fourth and most contemporary point of view, Dougherty's "relative autonomy of the state" perspective, to analyze a U.S. Department of Education report titled *The 21st Century Community College: A Strategic Guide to Maximizing Labor Market Responsiveness*. I discuss key elements of the document, and in the end I argue that federal agencies use their influence to effect change in the culture and curriculum of public colleges.

Explanations for the Move toward Job Training

The first authors to comment on the trend were advocates. They suggested that workforce development programs grew in response to students' demands and parents' requests for practical courses (Medsker, 1960; Gleazer, 1969). The claim that students are responsible for the change is open to question, however.

Wolf suggests young people do not possess, "a detailed grasp of labor market trends," and thus could not have known what to ask for, specifically (2002, p. 85). She also raises a question from the standpoint of parents with college-aged children. Wolf asks readers to consider whether they would advise their own sons or daughters to "abandon general education in favor of training which leads to a specific trade—when that trade itself may disappear tomorrow?" (Wolf, 2002, p. 85). The collective answer is, no.

Furthermore, retrospective studies demonstrate that colleges established vocational programs before demand arose. If we define student demand as enrollment in vocational courses, we face the fact that "these enrollments did not precede or accompany, but come well after the first efforts by policymakers to vocationalize the community college" (Dougherty, 2001, p. 239). In other words, student demand could not have caused the shift toward labor force development, leaving questions such as, "Why occupational programs?" and "For whom?" unanswered.

The second group of authors to address the questions viewed them through the lens of critical theory. They charged that occupationalism resulted from a desire on the part of multinational corporations to have their training costs subsidized by taxpayers (Bowles and Gintis, 1976; Zwerling, 1976; Pincus, 1980). Critics also claimed that vocational programs have the undesirable effect of tracking lower middle-class students into lower middle-class jobs, thus reproducing the social hierarchy (Bourdieu and Passeron, 1977). Although critical scholars published the bulk of their work in the 1970s, current research supports the claim that students from families with modest incomes are likely to enroll in job-training programs as opposed to the arts or sciences (Goyette and Mullen, 2006). Recent studies also demonstrate that students on the vocational track fair less well than their peers on the measure of long-term educational achievement (Alfonso, Bailey, and Scott, 2004).

In the wake of criticisms implicating corporations in the shift toward labor force development, a third group of authors considered the influence of business leaders on curriculum. Yet, in a comprehensive historical study, Brint and Karabel demonstrated that, like students, business people expressed little interest in the training programs rising to prominence in two-year colleges (1989). Dougherty addressed the same issue and came to the same conclusion (1994). He suggested that business leaders often participated in local efforts to expand vocational offerings, but he also noted that two-year schools vocationalized, "well before extensive business pressure first appeared," and he continued to add that, "business's participation has been at best moderate at the state level and nonexistent at the national level" (1994, p. 239). Businesses have a stake in the idea that community colleges act as public entities that are responsive to the wishes of the private sector, but multiple sources suggest that business leaders played a minimal role in vocationalizing colleges.

In *The Diverted Dream*, Brint and Karabel posed an alternative, "institutional" explanation for the shift to occupational programs (1989). They suggested that administrators came to see job training as a means of ensuring their organization's survival. Prior to vocationalization:

> Community colleges, by their very location in the structure of higher education, were badly situated to compete with better-established institutions. The best that community colleges could do, therefore, was to try to situate themselves favorably for the next available market niche. Therein resided the powerful organizational appeal for the two-year college's long-standing vocationalization project. (Brint and Karabel, 1989, p. 16-17)

Brint and Karabel proposed that vocational programs satisfied the organizational interests of community colleges by capturing a segment of the student body that was thought to be ignored by baccalaureate-granting schools. Dougherty concurred, but he also claimed the efforts of institutional actors only provide a partial explanation for the shift toward occupational training. In his words, "institutional theory does not give an equally central role to state governors, legislators, chief school officers, U.S. presidents, and members of Congress, even though they were also master voca-tionalizers" (1994, p. 34). For an understanding of the role that government officials played in the process of shifting the focus of two-year schools toward job training, Dougherty introduced a new perspective to the literature on the two-year college: "relative autonomy of the state" (1994).

Relative Autonomy of the State

In his landmark work, *The Contradictory College*, Dougherty explains how community colleges were driven to vocationalize in large part due to the influence of individuals and agencies in local, state, and federal government (1994). In his words, "The 'state relative autonomy' argument puts the autonomous—but only relatively autonomous—actions of government officials at the heart of the explanation of the rise of vocationalization" (1994, p. 36). Dougherty highlights the "relative" autonomy of state officials because they operate under conditions of subtle, but meaningful, limitation. For instance, candidates for public office depend on the private sector for resources and finances. While they are dependent on private streams of revenue, their actions bend toward the interests of those in positions to contrib-ute to campaigns (Pfeffer and Salancik, 1978). Public officials make autonomous decisions, but they do so in the context of dependence on capital generated in the marketplace (Aldrich and Pfeffer, 1976).

For example, "business controls the capital investment decisions that drive economic growth," and as a result, "one way governors have tried to pry that capital loose has been to offer business an attractive carrot: publicly subsidized employment training through the community college" (Dougherty, 1994, p. 28). In addition, the argument suggests that government officials share the ideol-ogy of the groups that they depend upon. Thus, their actions are reduced to serving private sector interests, as opposed to shielding citizens from hardship or the volatility of the market (DiMaggio and Powell, 1983).

In the case of resource dependence, the influence on officials is tangible and quantifiable, but the ideology pressing on public servants is less clear and seldom studied. When scholars write about the influence of government agencies they often avoid discussions of "the individual and organizational *self-interests* and *values* that help animate public officials' actions" (Dougherty, 1994, p. 283). As a case in point, research on the community college rarely includes reference to the beliefs and values that give shape to state officials' prescriptions for policy or practice. In what follows, I draw upon the work of Ayers (2005), Labaree (1997) and others in an analysis of the ideology ingrained within *The 21st Century Community College: A Strategic Guide to Maximizing Labor Market Responsiveness* (U.S. Department of Education, 2004).

The Twenty-First Century Community College

In September of 2004, the U.S. Department of Education released a report on *The 21st Century Community College*. In analyzing the report, it is crucial to note that non-elected officials, such as those employed by the U.S. Department of Education, present a different case than elected officials on the subject of resource dependence. Politicians depend directly on the private sector, but non-elected officials are interested in "protecting their position by increasing their agency's power, organizational status, and appropriations," and according to Dougherty, they do so through a process of pressuring their superiors by "establishing alliances with private interest groups" (1994, p. 285). *The 21st Century Community College* serves as a showcase of the techniques non-elected officials use to forge alliances with organizations in the private sector, thereby winning favor with superiors.

Throughout the report, there are attempts to establish a rapport with businesses. The most obvious are claims to the effect that two-year schools hold the potential to become "engines of economic development" (U.S. Department of Education, 2004, p. 1). Signs of resource dependence are steady and frequent in the document, but in what follows I adhere to Dougherty's suggestion to consider the ideology that justifies the program for change prescribed by officials.

In the case of *The 21st Century Community College*, the suggestion to focus on ideology is appropriate, because the report is not a work of science or scholarship. In the preface to the document, the authors make it plain that, "This report does not represent findings from an experimentally designed study carried out in a controlled setting" (p. v). Instead, the report is a set of suggestions drawn from a sample of more than thirty colleges, chosen for their prescient attempts at market responsiveness. The intent of the document is to encourage leaders to "take action" (p. v).

The authors claim the exclusive focus on schools devoted to market responsiveness is apt, as "this is a new area of study, and no preliminary analysis has been conducted that was ready to be subjected to a more rigorous research design," but the claim is difficult to accept (p. v). The vocationalization of the community college has been discussed at some length in the literature on postsecondary schools (Clark, 1960; Zwerling, 1976; Karabel, 1980; Pincus, 1980; Cohen and Brawer, 1982; Frye, 1994; Grubb, 1996; Labaree, 1997; Schuyler, 1999; Levin, 2001; Bragg, 2001; Brint, 2003).

The freedom to circumvent a large body of scholarly work is one aspect of the autonomy enjoyed by federal employees. As non-academics, government agency officials are not bound by the tradition of reviewing literature. Of course, U.S. Department of Education staff consult and reference the literature on public institutions (Adelman, 2005) but they are also free to generate suggestions for policy or practice independent of research or scholarship.

The authors of *The 21st Century Community College* make the most of their impunity from academic norms, but the authors also suggest two-year school professionals should act with a similar level of autonomy. The authors propose that a successful college "does not simply respond to needs" in a community as uncovered by research or needs assessments (Drury, 2001, p. 6). Rather, they suggest an effective college "creates conditions that demand its services" (Drury, 2001, p. 6). In these terms, market responsiveness becomes a goal in and of itself. The authors advise college leaders to create a demand for market responsiveness, even in areas where such a demand does not exist. The suggestion signals a break with academic or data-driven decision making, and entry into a realm of practice shaped by adherence to free-market values.

The authors offer community college leaders a number of steps to follow in the transformation to labor market responsiveness. The steps include suggestions for fund raising, strategic planning, and partnership building. But two themes hold a constant presence in the report, and both are consistent with the demand to structure schools on lines that make educational goals subordinate to business interests. The first theme centers on raising the status of noncredit vocational classes, so they enjoy the same level of esteem attached to traditional college courses. The second theme is focused on involving employers in decisions about curriculum.

The Ascendance of Noncredit Coursework

Throughout the report the authors display an aversion to the traditions of the academy, and they recommend raising the status of noncredit vocational classes up alongside of courses offered for college credit. Specifically, the authors ask administrators to initiate a change in the perception of noncredit job-training programs. In their words, "A cultural shift is required to ensure that all forms of learning, whether in credit classes or not, are viewed as equally important" (U.S. Department of Education, 2004, p. 14).

In the process of promoting noncredit classes, the authors of the report propose, "The flexibility of the noncredit division allows the quick creation of new courses that respond to immediate needs," and they offer an incentive to colleges by hinting at the potential for organizational growth (2004, p. 16). They suggest enrollment can grow in noncredit courses, "while credit programs are seeking approval from academic departments and from the college" (2004, p. 16). In other words, within the authors' belief system, institutional growth is valued more highly than democratic processes or faculty ownership of the curriculum. While it may be true that noncredit courses are consistent with the financial interests of colleges and businesses, the authors go on to suggest that students also benefit from an increased number of noncredit programs, and that claim rests on tenuous assumptions.

In an exhibit of their zeal for noncredit classes, the authors of the report bemoan the fact that community colleges in affluent areas "often face a high demand for programs geared toward students looking to transfer to a four-year institution," but they suggest a campus "in a predominately blue-collar community has an advantage, because such populations are more likely to seek training in order to gain employment" (2004, p. 18). Thus, the goal is to remake the community college in the image of vocational institutes. Working-class people are simply seen as a means to achieve those ends. The question of whether occupational programs serve the long-term interests of low-income students is not addressed, and it could be argued that students from blue-collar cities and towns deserve institutions of the same type as those found in upscale locations.

Labaree suggests the attempt to offer disadvantaged students noncredit courses and programs, with the hope of changing the perception of those programs in American culture, is a "loser's strategy" (1997, p. 220). When the interests of disadvantaged students are a concern, the best strategy is not to change the way noncredit courses with short-term utility are perceived in the eyes of the public. The struggle is to ensure that all students take part in a program of coursework that grants them credit and credentials that are portable from one location and one career to another, while sustaining long-term cultural worth. In Labaree's terms, "the way for a college to provide students with an edge in the race for status attainment is to give them credentials that have a high exchange value" (1997, p. 220). There is recent evidence to suggest that select occupational programs generate high income in the short term (Bragg, 2001, Carnevale, 2008), but in the long run community colleges do not serve underprivileged students by urging them toward narrow vocational programs in lieu of associate degrees or feasible paths to the baccalaureate.

Faculty, Industry, and the Curriculum

The authors of *The 21st Century Community College* recognize that, "the culture of higher education has asserted that faculty members are the most knowledgeable about course design and development" (2004, p. 25). But they break with tradition by pressing for the creation of a scenario in which, "business and industry representatives are brought in at the beginning" to make certain that lesson plans are tailored to their interests (2004, p. 25). In order to assure that corporations are involved in course creation at the same level as faculty, the authors prescribe the use of what is called a DACUM process (shorthand for Developing-a-Curriculum). DACUM is a proprietary, competency-based curriculum framework, available through the Center on Education and Training for Employment at Ohio State University (Norton, 1998).

When faculty engage in the DACUM process, they work directly with employees. They ask workers to reduce their jobs to a series of verifiable steps. The DACUM process unfolds in the act of describing the tasks employees perform on the job (Norton, 1998). If faculty follow the steps in the DACUM process, the end result is a list of chores, unique to an employer, that students complete as a way to demonstrate their competence.

Ayers suggests that when faculty cater curriculum to the demands of employers, they abandon their commitment to "community-based programming" (2005, p. 537) and as a result, the interests of capital are placed ahead of state or national goals.

In addition, when colleges adopt a curriculum model where the objectives are set by companies, the role of the faculty member is reduced to that of an automaton. The profession of teaching is reduced to merely running a series of drills, tailored to the interests of businesses in the position to hire graduates. The arrangement can be unsettling for faculty, but in the push to subsidize training costs, teachers are pressed to comply with demands for market responsiveness, to the point where the pressures manifest themselves as threats.

In order to ensure that faculty and staff accept terms and conditions consistent with the theme of responding to shifts in the economy, the authors describe a strategy for inculcating market values. They offer a technique used by Moraine Valley Community College as an example of the model that they recommend. At Moraine Valley, "staff members are peppered with language" (2004, p. 23). Administrators drill employees with words and phrases, like "seamlessness" and "web of inclusiveness," to remind teachers that their efforts in the classroom are to be structured in relation to the interests of businesses (U.S. Department of Education, 2004, p. 23). The practice of peppering educators with the language of the market proved successful. In the words of one staff member, "People here talk like that. We live it" (U.S. Department of Education, 2004, p. 23). But at Moraine Valley, and there is reason to believe at other colleges, a different message also accompanies the shift to market responsiveness. The message is, "You're either on board or you go away" (U.S. Department of Education, 2004, p. 23).

The approach is not subtle. A question remains, however. To what degree should public schools use tax dollars to train students to specifications set by employers? According to Wolf, "Specific training is defined as training which is relevant to a particular company," and when skills or abilities are unique to a business, "it makes sense for employers to pay for this, just as for new machinery, because they can expect to reap the benefit when they sell the output" (2002, p. 134).

Even so, despite Wolf's logic, it is no surprise to find government officials promoting subsidized training to organizations that they think of as constituents. The relative autonomy of the state perspective draws attention to the process by which officials become dependent upon and, therefore, likely to serve what they perceive to be the interests of the private sector (Dougherty, 1994).

The twenty-first century represents a new era for both U.S. and international businesses, however. There is evidence to suggest that the liberal arts are more than just a means to foster student development and enrich the cultural life of the nation. The liberal arts are also economically viable. In contrast to earlier eras where a set of skills were of long-term value in the workplace, today "the common pattern is one of frequent job changes and job redefinition," and in such an environment specific skills are less valuable than general capacities (Wolf, 2002, p. 153). Ironically, "the best preparation for the work of the future might be to cultivate knowledge of the broadest possible kind," and current research supports the notion that the liberal arts are valued in the labor force (Aronowitz, 2002, p. 161). Drawing on a 2001 report from the Business-Higher Education Forum, a collaboration between the American Council on Education and the National Alliance of Business, Newman, Couturier and Scurry note that current job descriptions call for "cross-functional skills, including leadership, teamwork, problem solving, analytical thinking, global consciousness, and reading and writing;" goals associated with the arts and sciences (2004, p. 73).

Conclusion

Historians suggest the move to vocationalize the American community college was not driven by the long-term interests of students or broad social and cultural goals. Likewise, the shift to vocational programs was not predicated on a foundation of research aimed at understanding how to increase economic parity, political engagement or community participation. Instead, the culture of market responsiveness grew in the wake of a desire on the part of public officials to enamor the private sector, although, evidence suggests that narrow training programs may be out of step with the demands of a post-industrial economy.

Throughout *The 21st Century Community College* the authors offer signs that they are aware their prescription for change is controversial, contrary to the purpose of public colleges, and likely to meet with resistance. In a section of the report titled "Common Barriers to Market Responsiveness" the authors suggest that faculty often cling to the idea that their goals are, "traditional and academically oriented" (2004, p. 15). The authors presume that attempts to wrest control of the curriculum from teachers will meet with opposition, but it is unclear whether faculty can mount a challenge to the practice or ideology of vocationalism. Both critics and advocates agree that the focus moved from the liberal arts to job training, and the change came about with a surprising lack of resistance.

According to Engel, the success of the movement to vocationalize is due, at least in part, to "ideological confusion among many of those who might chart a different path" (2000, p. 5). He suggests, "They have accepted the language and criteria of market ideology themselves" (2000, p. 5). With the hope of providing low-income students with access to careers, faculty and staff begin to concede that two-year schools exist to pursue goals that are purely economic or utilitarian. For example, in a case study of seven community colleges in both the U.S. and Canada, Levin found that "government policy in the 1990s clearly favored the interests of business, industry, and capital," and to the extent that government officials promoted business interests, college staff gave minimal attention to issues of "equity, access, and an informed citizenry—issues that could be held up as critical to the community college movement" (Levin, 2001, p. 112). In the 1990s, staff and faculty altered their beliefs and practices to match an agenda crafted by agencies such as the U.S. Department of Education, and the trend continues in this century.

If two-year schools are to readdress themselves to issues of justice or equality, and if they are to become a civic or moral force in society, as opposed to simply serving the interests of capital, educators must give thought to the roles filled by their institutions. Then they must assert themselves in college governance. In *The 21st Century Community College*, there rests an assumption that administrators are to drive the turn away from the liberal arts and toward workforce development. The change in organizational culture prescribed by the authors is not meant to come about through deliberation. Still, there is strong support for the tradition of shared governance in higher education, and democratic processes are insisted upon by accrediting agencies.

In *The 21st Century Community College*, market responsiveness means more than tailoring curriculum or teaching methods to the changing economy. The authors ask colleges to abandon the traditions of academia—research, open dialogue, and democratic governance—in order to align their norms and values with those of the marketplace. The twenty-first century is young, however, and the future of the community college is, as it has always been, in a state of flux. Therefore, two-year school professionals would do well to discuss the social and cultural purpose of their work. Business interests have a place in the discussion, as they have a stake in the future of the institution, but the voice of the private sector is not the sole voice to be heard. There are public purposes for citizens, educators and officials to consider in the process of setting a course for two-year colleges.

Even so, there are strong organizations that work to keep staff and faculty from considering a broad public agenda for their schools. At the national level, the American Association of Community Colleges (AACC) determines institutional priorities. Over the course of its history, the group demonstrated a preference for promoting short-term technical programs. In the chapter that follows, I examine the beliefs and values that guided the AACC's actions.

The association's history serves as an example of how social and economic forces coalesce to influence groups with the function of steering educational policy, and the organization's recent practices illustrate how national networks effect change with implications that reach all the way down into the classroom.

5

Professional Organizations: The American Association of Community Colleges

Founded in 1920, the American Association of Community Colleges has served as a leading advocate and national voice for two-year colleges. The organization counts 95 percent of all two-year schools as members, and the group represents approximately ten million students. The association is remarkable from the standpoint of its size and scope, but AACC history and culture receive little in the way of scholarly attention. For an association with the expressed purpose of steering policy and influencing schools, there is a surprising lack of research aimed at understanding the implications of the AACC's actions.

Intermediary Organizations

The association serves as an example of what are increasingly called "intermediary organizations" (Honig, 2004; Metcalf, 2005). According to Metcalf, intermediary organizations are agencies that situate themselves between industry, education, and state or federal governments (2005). The organizations function by creating a space where representatives from public and private entities can "meet, discuss mutually supportive goals, and strategize ways to achieve those goals" (Metcalf, 2005, p. 16). For example, in February of 2007, the AACC hosted a Workforce Development Institute in San Diego, California. More than four hundred groups and individuals participated, among them "thirty community college presidents, representatives from government agencies, and business leaders" (www.aacc.nche.edu, 6/4/07). The schedule included presentations on topics related to the role of colleges in communities, subjects such as service learning for example, but the bulk of the seminars focused on labor force development.

As an intermediary organization, the AACC creates a forum through which government agencies and private industries share perspectives. In turn, organizations in both the public and private sectors fund the association through grants, membership dues, and sponsorships (Metcalf, 2005). At the time of the Workforce Development Institute, the AACC's top contributors included The Coca-Cola Company, IBM, Sallie Mae, and Datatel Incorporated (www.aacc.nche.edu, 6/4/07).

In the past, when scholars made efforts to understand the external forces that influence the community college, they turned to institutional actors (Brint and Karabel, 1989), businesses (Levin, 2001), or government agencies (Dougherty, 1994) leaving intermediary organizations free from scrutiny. In this chapter, I draw upon the work of Brick (1963), Goodwin (1973), Labaree (1997) and others in an examination of the AACC's history, culture, and contemporary practices. Through an analysis of the association's efforts, it can be shown that the organization has participated in attempts to shape the identity and define the institutional logic of two-year schools, for better and for worse, over the course of its history.

AACC Culture and Values

The American Association of Community Colleges came into existence during the early part of the twentieth century, the period when two-year colleges started to proliferate. Prior to the founding of the AACC (known in the beginning as the American Association of Junior Colleges) two-year schools were a group of loosely related institutions with similar mission statements. At the time, however, two-year college educators and administrators concluded that the schools needed a national body to serve as a conduit for communication and to act as a nationwide representative. In effect, the association was born out of an attempt to define the two-year college within the context of American culture. In the words of AACC historian Michael Brick, "The Association acted as spokesman—telling the junior college story to the government, to educational organizations, to the public, and to its administrators and faculty" (Brick, 1963, p. 89).

From the perspective of AACC members, however, the story of the two-year college could not compel widespread support or admiration. In the early years of the twentieth century, two-year schools offered liberal arts subjects to local students, and that purpose seemed too restrictive to those participating in the community college movement. From the beginning, faculty members and administrators imagined something other than the tradition of offering courses in the arts and sciences. AACC members were uncomfortable with the thought that two-year schools limited themselves to simply transferring students to senior institutions, and they began to conceive a different mission and alternative role for community colleges.

The association began to promote a terminal two-year curriculum early in its history. AACC leaders favored vocational training programs to the degree that, "hardly a meeting throughout the 1920s and 1930s failed to discuss terminal education" (Brick, 1963, p. 120). The group assumed the schools needed to forge a unique market niche in order to thrive, and a consensus formed around the notion that the niche should differ from that of baccalaureate granting schools. Thus, the AACC worked to "temper the liberal arts attitude" of two-year colleges (Brick, 1963, p. 119).

Association members also saw job training as a means to advance the cause of American business. From the AACC's standpoint, "A highly industrial society demanded education for professions and vocations" (Brick, 1963, p. 110). In the minds of the association's leadership, the demands of the new society "modified the early focus on intellectual concerns" (Brick, 1963, p. 110). In contrast to four-year college and university administrators, who saw curriculum as the province of faculty members, community college leaders saw the curriculum "as a product of the society in which it operates," and as such they assumed that "educators have to analyze society and develop programs that respond to societal demands" (Brick, 1963, p. 112). Yet, the historical record is plain, the demands the AACC wished to respond to were less than societal. They were economic.

Throughout the nineteenth century, Americans concerned themselves with aesthetic, moral, political, and spiritual goals (Lasch, 2001) but by the turn of the twentieth century attention shifted toward commerce. AACC leaders were attuned to the norms and values of the day, and they maintained an outlook that matched the business-minded, albeit Darwinist spirit of the age. They conceived public education as a means for individuals to demonstrate their "fitness" or capacity for success, and they saw colleges as a mechanism for the nation to sort itself into classes. Brick offers the following as a summary of the beliefs central to the philosophy that justified the AACC's actions. He describes the beliefs as "the business way."

> Between 1865 and the present, a major element in American social thought defined itself. This element was "the business way" which held as principal ideas: (1) Material success comes as the reward of superior virtue, (2) there is an insignificant amount of social injustice in the existing society, (3) the fittest and best survive the tests of our society, and (4) wealth tends to be socially benevolent. (1963, p. 6)

In an era where social and economic inequality grew, the leaders of the AACC moved to align their organization with the interests of industrialists. They worked to craft a public institution with the intent to insulate those with wealth from academic criticism or reproach from the students who would become their employees. In the words of Goodwin:

> These educational leaders knew the kind of world they wanted—a world that would be orderly, efficient, and productive, and they knew the type of man they wished to mold—a man with the social conscience to blend harmoniously into the community and with the skills to perform his proper role at his proper level. (1973, p. 13)

The early efforts of the AACC were driven by the desire to establish a sense of efficiency and order in society. The AACC worked to change the role of the two-year college from one associated with the liberal arts, to one of producing a quiet and capable workforce, made up of employees willing to accept those in positions of authority as superiors. If such a labor force were developed, it was argued, "It could reduce possible friction between the educated elite and the masses" (Goodwin, 1973, p. 13). AACC officers made it their goal to create an institution consistent with the orderly and hierarchical society they considered ideal. In short, "These leaders looked to the community college as a social panacea" (Goodwin, 1973, p. 13).

The Legacy

The AACC succeeded in its effort to transform the two-year college into an instrument of labor force development. It was not a quick or easy transformation, however. In the beginning, academics resisted the turn away from the liberal arts. Brick explains, with respect to the United States, "Ours is a society which has achieved affluence through technology, yet it has traditionally looked down upon education that is not liberally oriented" (Brick, 1963, p. 188). In the early to middle twentieth century, academics and vocational educators clashed over questions about the content and the character of the college curriculum. Brick describes the debate as, "The conflict between culture and cash" (Brick, 1963, p. 112), but within the association there was no such controversy. The group's values and decisions favored the cash side of the conflict.

Throughout its history, the AACC pursued an agenda consistent with social stability as opposed to change. In effect, the association sought to preserve the social and economic disparity characteristic of the early twentieth century. Goodwin suggests, despite regular claims about innovation, "the community college movement stands as a profoundly conservative movement" (1973, p. 15). The community college's sole national advocacy group shifted the institution away from the liberal arts and the potential to unify the nation around a curriculum meant to provide every student with equal access to the finer things in life—art, history, music, philosophy, science, and literature. With respect to the AACC's agenda, Goodwin explains that their plans for the educational system were to transform it, "from the 'great equalizer' to the 'great selector' of society" (1973, p. 88). When colleges moved to make job training a priority, marginalized groups lost access to the rich cultural traditions imparted through the baccalaureate.

For organizational reasons, the AACC promoted a curriculum that distinguished community colleges from other institutions, and in the process the association played a part in the creation of a postsecondary network marked by difference and hierarchy, as opposed to equality and a curriculum uniformly devoted to the development of an engaged and competent citizenry. As a result, "The system has become better at creating invidious distinctions among students than at providing them with the social and political capacities" required for a healthy and productive civic life or public sphere (Labaree, 1997, p. 250).

The Twenty-First-Century Agenda

The AACC succeeded in its long-standing effort to reconstitute the community college as an institution devoted to workforce development, but the values espoused by the association are not universally shared. At least historically, colleges have been torn by conflicting mandates; one that says their role is to produce trained employees, and the other that says their goals is to educate citizens (Schultz, 2005). Thus, out of necessity the AACC has maintained an active calendar of events with the intent to continually promote the occupational curriculum. The events include "intra-professional discourses…official publications…and celebratory and developmental programs" (Greenwood, Suddaby, and Hinings, 2002, p. 74). Since the liberal arts and education for citizenship are valued in American culture, each event, publication, and program is undertaken with the goal of steering colleges toward economic goals.

For example, in 2003 and 2004 the association collaborated with the Center for Workforce Preparation (CWP) a division of the U.S. Chamber of Commerce, to host a series of regional dialogues. The dialogues brought community college professionals into contact with business leaders and Chamber of Commerce officials. The intent of the forums was to, "Identify, evaluate, and select promising practices that will build the capacity of chambers of commerce and community colleges to develop the workforce" (CWP and AACC, 2003a, p. 1). Reports published after each event serve as summaries of the discussions that took place during the forums. In the reports, it is suggested that the dialogues aimed to increase the chance that chambers of commerce, community colleges, and businesses work together to form arrangements that they find mutually beneficial.

The discussions were held as half-day sessions in the cities of Chicago, Seattle, New Orleans, and Schnecksville, Pennsylvania. Approximately thirty participants attended each forum, and according to the AACC's executive summaries, "Participants were asked to respond to a series of questions about what new values and attitudes they see in market-responsive community college systems, what types of relationships they envision, and what effects these systems have on the community" (CWP and AACC, 2003a, p. 3).

Intermediary organizations host forums where members of diverse groups engage in dialogue. The interaction takes place around a set of purposefully chosen questions, and the conversation affirms norms that participants observe and then take with them when they return to their places of employment. In a study of the impact of professional associations on the beliefs and values of practitioners, Greenwood, Suddaby and Hinings explain:

> Associations can legitimate change by hosting a process of discourse through which change is debated and endorsed: first by negotiating and managing the debate within the profession; and, second, by reframing professional identities as they are represented to others outside the profession. (2002, p. 59)

The forums held across the country afforded two-year school professionals a chance to negotiate answers to questions about the economic roles fulfilled by colleges. In other words, the AACC used its position to bring college leaders together with business people in a forum where the conversations oriented participants toward commercial objectives. It is within the context of such settings that identities are shaped and values are shared. Dialogues such as those hosted by the AACC and the CWP create forums where professional roles are defined and goals are constructed.

In what follows, I offer a sample of the comments recorded by AACC staff during the half-day sessions. The comments were presented in a series of publications titled *Building Market Driven Systems: A National Dialogue* (CWP and AACC, 2003a, 2003b, 2003c, 2004). I chose remarks from the reports with the intent to illustrate the overall tenor and content of the discourse. Participants made the following statements:

- The market-responsive community college system generates credible, reliable, and appropriately skilled product for employers (2003b, p. 6).

- Community colleges develop a curriculum in partnership with businesses (2003a, p. 5).

- Community colleges reach out to local business regularly and research what those business needs are in the community (2003c, p. 9).

- Students are receiving "real world" training by industry experts through the market-responsive community college system (2003c, p. 11).

- The community college system is marked by a much more aggressive business outreach function (2003c, p. 13).

- Community colleges serve local businesses and provide customized rapid response to training needs (2004, p. 9).

- Community colleges blend the lines between credit and noncredit courses (2003b, p. 5).

- Community colleges train students based on business needs (2003a, p .4).

- Community colleges place emphasis on customized short-term training needs to meet industry demands (2004, p. 9).

According to Greenwood, Suddaby, and Hinings, professional associations work to create social arenas where ideas or notions about the goals of the profession can be steered in a direction the group considers desirable. They refer to the process as one of "theorization" (2002). In their words, "Theorization is integral to institutional change. It is the rendering of ideas into understandable and compelling formats" (2002, p. 75). In this case, participants worked to answer the prescribed questions in such a way as to incite one another to see the goals of educators and business people as compatible.

Since it is widely known that the vocationalization of community colleges has been achieved, one might wonder whether such attempts at professional socialization are necessary, but intermediary organizations with an interest in steering public institutions toward serving the interests of businesses must maintain a constant vigil. Even though the majority of community college professionals accept the workforce training agenda as a legitimate set of objectives for higher education, there remains a lengthy history of dedication to broader and more humanistic goals. That history and those goals have to be routinely theorized out of existence or at least minimized to the point where they do not present a threat to the new vocationalism. Greenwood, Suddaby, and Hinings suggest:

> The importance of theorization is likely to be especially acute in mature, highly professional settings, where the boundaries of occupational communities and the templates of appropriate organizational forms are established and structured. (2002, p. 61)

College teaching is an old profession, constituted by an autonomous group of practitioners. Thus, the steps that must be taken to shape educators' views and goals are substantial. If the process of theorization is successful, then the ideas valued by the intermediary organization, "become taken-for-granted" and the desired objectives and structures come to be seen as a "natural and appropriate arrangement" (Greenwood, Suddaby, and Hinings, 2002, p. 61).

The AACC succeeded in its effort to bind the work of educators to goals consistent with the objectives of the U.S. Chamber of Commerce. In all four of the reports from the *National Dialogues*, and in more than forty pages of commentary, there are only two remarks that broach the subject of the liberal arts, and in both cases, the comments are couched in terms of the value general education stands to generate in the labor force.

For example, during the Seattle meeting, one of the participants made the point that, "Community colleges are not ignoring the vital role of a liberal arts education, but making it more relevant to careers" (CWP and AACC, 2003c, p. 13). Similarly, in New Orleans, a participant remarked that, "Ethics and character building are part of the curriculum offered at community colleges," but the person qualified the statement by suggesting that ethics and character development, "help students succeed in the workplace" (CWP and AACC, 2004, p. 9). Of course, ethics and character are helpful in the labor market. But economic success is not the only reason to value character development, and a strong foundation in ethics is as useful when it comes to challenging conventional business practices as it is in furthering careers.

Conclusion

Perched in the intermediary terrain between government agencies, industry, and higher education, the American Association of Community Colleges found itself engaged in larger social, political and economic struggles over the course of the twentieth century. "The history of the community college suggests that the tension between politics and markets played itself out—as a broad-based struggle for institutional control between democratic and capitalist goals" (Labaree, 1997, p. 218). The AACC did not play the role of a neutral bystander in the debate over whether two-year schools should serve public purposes or narrow private interests, however.

And today the outcome is clear—fiscal pressures and market ideology trumped the public interest in the community college.

Dialogues such as those hosted by the AACC and the CWP exert influence on the norms and values that govern life in two-year schools. When the AACC has been able to make the most of its position as an intermediary, the group has used its members and staff to strengthen the bond between public schools and private businesses. Historically, the organization's leadership assumed that both groups were served in the process.

From the standpoint of the organization's members, one might argue that AACC officers acted in a manner consistent with their understanding of what is best for community colleges. Certainly, two-year schools grew and prospered under the AACC's benefaction. One might even conclude that the AACC's efforts have been good for community colleges, but there is another, more important question to ask. Has the American Association of Community Colleges been good for America? Such a question is more difficult to answer. The reply has to bend in at least two different directions—the first is social and the second is economic.

The social cost of providing students of modest means with an education of a different type than one receives in the upper-middle class is substantial. During the time that community colleges have spent committing themselves to job training, the social distance between Americans has grown (Bishop and Cushing, 2008). Citizens have less in common today as a result of the changing postsecondary curriculum. In the public sphere, resentment grows between employees trained to perform a narrow set of job-related skills, and what are perceived to be a group of educated, cultural elites. The situation has escalated to the point where it makes community building a challenge and national conversations on topics of importance unlikely.

There are also economic consequences associated with the proliferation of job-training programs. Anthony Carnevale, director of the Global Institute on Education and the Economy at Georgetown

University, suggests, "The economic value of general competencies exceeds and is growing faster than job-specific competencies,"
and he goes on to add, "That is why managers and professionals
make more than technicians, even in high-tech firms" (2008, p. 29).
Yet, general education and the liberal arts continue to languor in
the community college, with low enrollments and a low sense of
institutional priority. The economic consequences of the shift are
significant to both individual students and the nation.

Students enroll in community colleges with the hope of immediate success in the job market, and when they land on campus,
instead of finding professionals capable of explaining the mul-
titudinous value of the liberal arts, they find staff, faculty, and
administrators that are willing to oblige their short-term interests.
That is due at least in part to the success of organizations such as
the AACC. The association has been so successful in shaping the
views and professional identities of two-year school practitioners,
teachers and counselors became willing to set aside their own
values and preferences when they work with students in the community college.

For example, when I have the opportunity to participate in
forums where college missions are discussed, I always make it a
point to ask colleagues advocating short-term training programs if
they have children. When I find parents I ask them when their sons
or daughters are expected to graduate from high school. After they
list their children's names and expected graduation dates, I say, "I
suppose they will stay home and work on a short-term, noncredit,
training regimen, maybe over the Internet?" The reactions differ.
Sometimes my colleagues explain in earnest that their children
have been planning to attend Ivy League universities since they
were in middle school. Other times the question prompts emotional
outbursts on such lines as these: "Hell no! My kids are going to a
real university and they're getting a real education!"

In the moments that follow, I am usually quiet. I offer a knowing
grin or a calculated nod. Sometimes the moment is poignant, and

other times the irony is lost, but in either case I come to the same conclusion. Job-training programs often sound like good ideas—as long as they are intended for someone else's son or daughter. The truth is they are less than desirable for any and all of our children. Public occupational training programs have served to perpetuate a society marked by intellectual inequality and economic polarization. Yet, vocational degrees and certificates with little, and in some cases no liberal arts components, have become the predominant form of education in two-year colleges.

In the next section I continue the analysis of entities that worked to undermine the liberal arts in two-year schools, but I do so in a different light. In the three chapters that follow, I offer suggestions for a renewed commitment to the arts and sciences—beginning with curriculum, moving on to organizational structure, and ending with a plan for improving classroom teaching strategies.

Part Three:

The Promise of the Arts and Sciences

6

Curriculum:
Localized and Problem-Based

The 1990s were watershed years in the move to globalize the community college, and the momentum continues into the present. Speakers visit campuses to promote the idea, colleges host conferences on the subject, and grant money allows teachers to add international components to their classes. Faculty leaders and administrators both remain committed to maintaining the two-year college as an institution with an international flavor.

In the latter part of the twentieth century, the American Association of Community Colleges made a strong attempt to encourage teachers to adopt international curricula. The AACC's efforts were successful. From the results of a 2001 survey returned by 307 institutions, Blair, Phinney, and Phillipe reported that "82 percent of the colleges offered international components in their classes, compared with 40 percent in 1995" (2001, p. 1). In addition, "the number of colleges with international business programs grew from 23 percent in 1995 to 60 percent in 2000" (Blair, Phinney, and Phillipe, 2001, p. 1).

In the beginning, I will admit I was drawn to the idea. Sociologists like to think of themselves as worldly characters, and as such, we are susceptible to movements that sound even vaguely cosmopolitan. But as I began to learn about the effort to globalize the community college, the initiative started to seem inconsistent with my approach to teaching, and as I developed a better understanding of the movement toward an international curriculum, I discovered the move is out of step with the goals of higher education.

In the social sciences, international perspectives and cross-cultural comparisons are commonplace. They are a regular part of our courses. Sociologists have long understood that students learn about themselves by comparing their beliefs and values to those of others. We call the strategy "seeing the strange in the familiar" (Macionis, 2007). We view American life through the lens of other cultures. For example, in courses on crime and delinquency, the difference between American and Japanese parenting techniques are often discussed. The Japanese approach to discipline includes a practice similar to "grounding," although, when Japanese kids are grounded, they are not allowed in the home with their parents or siblings (Barkan, 2004). By contrast, American children conceive time spent indoors as an infringement on their personal freedom, raising questions about how time spent with family came to be construed as punishment.

Comparisons such as these abound in social science, but in the push to globalize public colleges, the intent is not to use the perspectives of others to cast illuminating light on our own norms or conventions. In particular, supporters of the new curriculum are reluctant to use the views of others to raise questions about the actions or behaviors of international businesses. As I listened to speakers, and later as I read authors extolling the virtues of globalization, it became clear that the intent is to, "shape student thinking primarily with employers in mind" (Farnsworth, 2006, p. B17). In the new curriculum, little attention is paid to unfair labor practices or movements designed to strengthen environmental laws. Similarly, global education advocates are seldom interested in test questions or in-class activities centered on the practice of outsourcing U.S. jobs or the techniques corporations use to avoid paying taxes.

The move to adopt an international curriculum is driven by an eagerness to promote economic globalization. The movement's origins stem, not from educational theory or research on student development, but from needs that grew out of human resource departments in the private sector. Tow explains, "Corporate Personnel Directors say their companies need managers and employees with greater international knowledge and experience," and in response to the demand for employees familiar with the language and customs of others, community colleges altered their curriculum so as to curry favor with companies trading in the global market (2001, p. 30).

The upshot of the effort has been a surge of funds from government agencies and corporations, both attuned to the idea that colleges contribute to the economy by training students to use skills of value in the labor force. The move toward an international curriculum has been lucrative for colleges, but in the rush to transform the community college into a global institution, staff and faculty became inclined to adopt a naïve, uncritical, nearly cartoon-like appreciation for all things international. For example, in a 2001 article for the AACC's *Community College Journal*, Farnsworth suggests that international education holds the potential to change students to the point where their experience matches that of Dorothy, the main character from the film *The Wizard of Oz*. He recounts the moment in the picture when Dorothy is lifted from her community by a tornado:

> Dorothy is ripped away from the sparse black and white landscape of rural Kansas by the tornado. She spins through a whirlwind of confusing sights and sounds, drops with a jarring thud somewhere completely different. With her dog Toto under her arm, she hesitantly opens the monochrome door of the old farmhouse, and with a slight gasp ... walks into the glorious Technicolor world of Oz. (2001, p. 10)

Farnsworth goes on to connect the imagery of Oz to education, by suggesting, "Part of the learning process—of becoming an 'educated' person—now must involve opening the lives and minds of students to the wonders of the new Oz" (2001, p. 11). Societies marked by free trade agreements and inexpensive consumer goods are the new Oz to which the American Association of Community Colleges hopes to orient students. But global education of the kind promoted by the AACC lacks a sustained critique of world trade;

and if the dominant approach to the curriculum lacks a critical component, then the framework cannot facilitate critical thinking or critical literacy on the part of students.

In the literature published by the AACC, societies and cultures increasingly shaped by the advance of global capital are conceived as Oz-like worlds of "glorious Technicolor," but the image of magnificence and wonder stands in contrast to the picture of globalization painted by academics. University of Wisconsin sociologist Al Gedicks explains:

> From the Amazon Basin to the frozen stretches of northern Saskatchewan, to the tropical rainforests of Southeast Asia and Central Africa—energy, mining, logging, hydroelectric, and other mega-projects have uprooted, dislocated, and destroyed native communities. (1993, p. 13)

As public nonprofit institutions, community colleges are charged with an obligation to encourage students' social, moral, and identity development. Each form of development involves fostering students' skills in such a way that they can compare and assess competing points of view. The goal is to create a setting where students and teachers struggle to build a thorough understanding of human endeavors. "The deep purpose of higher education is to steward this transformation so that students and faculty together continually move from naiveté through skepticism to commitment" (Parks Dolaz, Keen, Keen, and Dolaz Parks, 1996, p. 12). Public colleges have a duty to move students away from credulity and toward a capacity to make judgments with respect to the merit and morality of the cultural patterns unfolding around them.

With respect to such patterns, any assessment of the business practices shaping life in modern societies makes it plain that the offices of international corporations are not staffed with cheery munchkins or well-intentioned fairies. In the case of global giants such as Enron the offices are no longer staffed at all, as the organization imploded in a flurry of greed and malevolence. Furthermore, of those organizations currently successful in the world market, an examination of their work reveals a widespread pattern of disregard for social problems that arise in the locales where they do business. In the parlance of international economics, persistent global poverty, geographic dislocation, and environmental degradation are described as "externalities." They are considered unintended consequences of trade, not central to the process of profit making.

The new world of global commerce may be wrought in Technicolor, it may even be glorious in some ways and for certain entities, but the faculty of public colleges have an obligation to evaluate international trade with a critical eye and from a range of different perspectives. Unfortunately, the international curriculum fell into place before faculty took time to stage a debate about its purpose. Community college teachers have yet to conduct a close examination of the assumptions that lie at the foundation of the new curriculum, and in the absence of deliberations on the intent or consequences of the new approach, staff and faculty simply came to believe that two-year schools exist to advance the cause of international business. With the wonders of inexpensive foreign-made goods dangled before us so as to produce an almost trance-like acceptance of the status quo, we find ourselves caught in the glow of international commerce, while matters of local concern smolder in our midst. For example, in the community college curriculum, we give scant attention to the battles waged by nonprofit organizations struggling to address the social and ecological problems that burgeon in the wake of economic "progress" (Stiglitz, 2002).

Consequently, in the spring of 2003 I presented a group of thirty-five students with a summary of a plan for drilling 50,000 new natural gas wells in Wyoming's Powder River Basin, thirty miles north of the Casper College campus (Beers, 2000; Lavelle, 2001). Students were dumbfounded. Some of them had spent time overseas in nations such as Germany, Sweden, and Guam as members of the military or as part of high school or college student exchange programs. On the whole, the group was well read and well traveled, but they were unaware of the effort to turn a portion of Wyoming's wide-open spaces into an industrial landscape at the hands of global companies. Should natural gas development go ahead as planned, the commercial activity will benefit multinational corporations based throughout the U.S., Europe, and Canada, while at the same time degrading American public land and trampling the geographic history and cultural values of long-time Wyoming residents (Duffy, 2005).

My students were initially outraged by the prospect of their home state's landscape becoming altered beyond recognition, and their passionate response to the threat posed by the new development fueled a lengthy in-class discussion about natural resources, consumer habits, and the stewardship of public land. Ideally, discussions such as these take place at meetings of the city council, the county commissioner, the state legislature, and in Federal offices. As an educator, I can only hope the perceptions and sentiments formed in the context of college courses reach beyond the classroom, off the campus, and into our communities. I am confident, in the case of this example, the discussion continues in other quarters. However, if I would have chosen a topic far removed from local concerns, I could rest assured the dialogue would have died as students stepped into the hallway after class.

For instance, I could have planned an activity focused on an international problem, such as deforestation in South America, but to do so would have kept students from the realization that global processes have present and immediate implications. Without a strong focus on local issues and social problems, international education places a mask over forces and events that impact communities. Moreover, when conducted in uncritical terms meant to glorify students' roles as consumers and employees, international education becomes apolitical, blinding students to their responsibilities as citizens.

As a case in point, in the spring of 2001 I asked a group of students in northern Wisconsin a question with respect to the public servants representing them in our democracy, but first I asked them to write the names of all the Green Bay Packer's players they knew or could remember. The lists were long. So lengthy, I was forced to give them more time than I planned. Roughly two-thirds of the students finished the roster. Those students then began writing the names of retired players or athletes placed on injured-reserve. After they finished, I asked them to write the names of the officials that represent them at the city, county, state, and federal levels. Three-fourths of the students were familiar with the governor, roughly one-half knew the city's mayor, a handful of students cited one of the two senators representing them in Washington, but the majority either sat silent or laughed out loud in the manner of people asked to perform a hopeless task.

My students are distracted from their duties as citizens in a self-governed society. They are not alone, however. Whether we are preoccupied with sports, work, television, or consumerism, the majority of us abrogate our role, our right, and our responsibility to play an active part in American public life (Putnam, 2000). Two-year colleges have the potential to serve as a hedge against the apathy that pervades our social and cultural networks. An engaged college classroom holds the promise of inspiring and empowering students to act upon the problems present in their localities. However, if the curriculum is centered on geographically distant themes, disconnected from communities, then college courses simply serve as additional distractions.

Higher education curriculum must include international perspectives—that much is understood—but the question is, "Global education for what purpose?" Currently, the international curriculum is aimed at equipping students with skills related to opening new labor markets (Tow, 2001; Farnsworth, 2006). The result of their work could well be a loss of jobs or a lower quality of life for neighbors and fellow citizens. By contrast, a genuine higher education provides students with the ability to conceive global commerce in terms of its multiple and wide-ranging effects: social, economic, and environmental.

A significant body of educational theory and research dating back to the work of John Dewey (1916) points toward the necessity of taking students from the local and particular, to the broad and general. Thus, from the standpoint of the two-year curriculum, the starting point is here at home, within our families, churches, schools, and neighborhoods. For both social and educational purposes, our in-class activities must be drawn from our vicinities; and if public colleges are going to play a role in the effort to reconnect education to communities, it is going to mean "establishing or re-establishing relationships with community groups—and not just businesses" (Gamson, 1997, p. 13).

Of course, classes and programs designed to spotlight local issues must eventually become regional if not global in scope. Responsible educators pay attention to "the patterns that connect the local and the regional with the global" (Orr, 1994, p. 160). But the intent is to create an environment where students develop the habit of analyzing local conditions from the standpoint of how they are influenced by international forces. After all, if community college students are not willing and equipped to address the social and economic problems in their own communities, then who will address them? The citizens of other nations? Foreign governments? Neither scenario seems likely or desirable.

In the preface to the 1983 Shocken Books edition of *Oz*, L. Frank Baum suggests of his story, "It aspires to being a modernized fairy tale, in which the wonderment and joy are retained and the heartaches and nightmares are left out" (Baum, 1983, p. xvi). Similarly, the effort to internationalize the community college has been an attempt to sell the joys and wonders of globalization, while drawing attention away from the "wars, pollution, starvation, species extinctions, and genocides" associated with the new international order (Perkins, 2004, p. 57). It was an easy sell. The spectacle of otherness is seductive for both students and faculty, but the one-sided focus on the benign aspects of globalization puts us in the undesirable position of advocating, as opposed to evaluating international business or global politics.

The literary critic Gore Vidal explains, "In sharp contrast to gray flat Kansas, Oz seems to blaze with color. Yet, the Emerald

City is a bit of a fraud. Everyone is obliged to wear green glasses in order to make the city appear emerald green" (1983, p. 258). In effect, by propagating uncritical pro-business international curricula, we are asking students to wear green glasses. Conversely, if colleges upheld their responsibility, the curriculum would function as a cold, clear microscope—classrooms serving as forums where global social and economic patterns could be assessed from the standpoint of human and ecological interests. In the light of clear and hard analysis, places like Kansas will seem less monochrome and more closely connected to global forces than students or faculty often imagine. Furthermore, if we put our communities back at the center of our efforts, students will likely come to see that, "There is no place like home," and that is a point upon which Dorothy and I agree.

A key advantage of the two-year college is that the institution provides local access to education, although the education students receive in two-year schools is increasingly of a different type than one finds in universities. In the chapter ahead, I discuss a small but growing movement within the community college—a move toward the baccalaureate.

7

Mission and Purpose: The Community College Baccalaureate

The community college stands at the apex of a curve, turning up into the high country of academia. Recently, governing bodies in Utah, Texas, Florida, Nevada, and Arkansas passed legislation granting formerly two-year schools the right to confer the baccalaureate. But despite the growing level of acceptance, four-year programs have engendered a debate among scholars, trustees, and lawmakers. The baccalaureate has both ardent supporters and a group of critics committed to questioning the place of four-year degrees in community colleges. Schools interested in creating bachelor's programs are praised for the attempt to serve students by new means, but at the same time they are also condemned as status seekers, stepping out of place in the postsecondary hierarchy.

In what follows, I consider the social and political issues pertinent to the debate on the community college baccalaureate. In the first phase of the analysis I examine the arguments, both in support of bachelor's degrees, and critical of four-year programs. In the second stage I discuss the baccalaureate within the context of community college history, and then I conclude with a call for teachers and scholars to conceive the schools in cultural terms. In contrast to work focused solely on the role of bachelor's degrees in the economy, I make a case for the community college baccalaureate as a step toward political equality and a renewed commitment to widespread civic engagement.

The Debate over the Baccalaureate

The debate over whether community colleges can or should develop baccalaureate programs takes place primarily in journalistic forums, such as the *Chronicle of Higher Education* and *Community College Week*. Thus far, questions have been raised with respect to whether baccalaureate programs are cost prohibitive (Eaton, 2005), whether they limit access to other educational services (Levin, 2004), whether community colleges are capable of providing upper-division courses of high quality (Wattenbarger, 2000), or whether four-year programs signal a shift of institutional identity (Townsend, 2005). Within the past thirty years, a small group of scholars raised larger questions about the role of the community college in society (Zwerling, 1976; Pincus, 1980; Brint and Karabel, 1989; Dougherty, 1994; Rhoads and Valdez, 1996), but the current debate is centered on practical concerns. The conversation is limited to questions about whether bachelor's degrees promote workforce development or contribute to students' economic well-being.

Critics of the move toward the baccalaureate suggest that degrees granted from community colleges are likely to be seen as "second-class," thereby hindering graduates in the job market (Wattenbarger, 2000; Eaton, 2005). The foundation of the claim is untenable, however. Associate degrees and short-term certificates suffer an even greater lack of prestige in relation to bachelor's degrees from four-year institutions, and low status did not keep two-year schools from successfully building and maintaining a wide range of sub-baccalaureate programs. On one hand, it is difficult to see why low status should keep community colleges from offering four-year credentials. On the other hand, it is fair to assume that status matters to students and employers—but if status is the issue—then the baccalaureate represents a chance for community colleges to rise up alongside well-respected institutions.

In contrast to critics, advocates champion four-year programs on the basis of the value they stand to generate in the workplace

(McKee, 2005). Supporters even suggest that community colleges should develop an "applied" or "workforce" bachelor's degree, tailored to the specific and ephemeral needs of corporations, and unmoored from the practices associated with "academic pedagogy" (Walker and Floyd, 2005, p. 96). Generally speaking, the arguments for and against the baccalaureate both turn on the question of whether the degree can serve as a vehicle for economic growth or personal mobility.

It is only when the conversation turns to the subject of institutional mission or identity that one finds a discussion of the social roles community colleges fulfill. Supporters and critics alike question the effect of the baccalaureate on the schools' overarching purpose, but critics stress this side of the argument. For example, one of the strongest objections to four-year programs is expressed when critics press the charge of "mission creep" (Mills, 2003). A small cadre of authors is concerned that colleges may shift attention and resources to bachelor's programs as they become more commonplace. In the process, they imply that colleges may neglect or short-change students that are not interested in the baccalaureate or deemed unfit for the degree. On this note, Levin issued a caveat:

> As long as the baccalaureate community college offers programs...such as special education programs for the mentally challenged, high school completion, and General Equivalency Diplomas (GED), and certificate vocational programs including welding, automotive, pipe-fitter, small appliance repair, and the like—then they will carry with them their traditional community college identity, which highlights open access and a comprehensive curriculum. (2004, p. 19)

Although a concern for underprivileged students clearly lies at the foundation of Levin's argument, it should be noted that the school's traditional identity was neither vocational nor comprehensive. It is true that the colleges were originally meant to serve groups that found it difficult to access education, but historically two-year colleges served the purpose of offering the freshman and sophomore years of bachelor's degrees. Roksa explains, "Community colleges originated as transfer institutions, with the majority of students participating in a four-year college preparatory curriculum" (2006, p. 501). Thus, one could argue, the real mission creep in the community college has been a long and slow but decisive creep away from the baccalaureate and toward narrow career-related associate degrees and certificate programs. Ironically, when community colleges crept *down* the ladder of prestige, the critics were silent.

Community Colleges and the History of Higher Education

The history of higher education is replete with change. Early American colleges patterned themselves on an English model emphasizing undergraduate education and character development, but in the middle twentieth-century, they adopted a research orientation similar to that of German institutions. For example, normal schools and teacher's colleges became state colleges and later comprehensive universities, as they added graduate schools and doctoral programs.

In the United States, institutional advancement occurred at all levels of the higher education network, except at the bottom. Over the course of its lifespan, the public community college clung to the lowest rung on the ladder. Scholars have examined the history of the community college and come to different conclusions about the cause of its stagnant character. Levin suggested that administrators favored occupational programs as a means to match their perception of workforce needs (2001); Dougherty documented the degree to which government agencies influenced the community college curriculum (1994); and Labaree explored the role of the American Association of Community Colleges (AACC) in setting a course for the institution (1997).

In the words of Labaree, "The community college was confined to the lowest rung on the ladder," because members of the AACC "wanted to see it remain a two-year institution and continue to play its vocational role," presumably, as a means to court students for whom bachelor's degrees seemed out of reach (1997, p. 192). As a result, the community college was kept from "following the same

trajectory of institutional mobility that had served its predecessors"
(Labaree, 1997, p. 192).

Although the influence of the AACC on particular schools un-
doubtedly varies, there is no question about the historical intent of
AACC leaders with respect to maintaining the community college
as a vocational institution. For example, after learning in 1929,
that 90 percent of community college students aspired to the baccalaureate, Walter Crosby Ells addressed the annual meeting of
the AACC as follows:

> It will be most unfortunate if the junior college becomes so successful as a popular-
> izing agency that it makes all of its students plan on full university courses. Probably
> the proportion of those continuing should be nearer fifty than ninety percent. This
> report of ninety percent is a distinct danger signal ahead. (Ells, quoted in Labaree,
> 1997, p. 201)

Community college leaders, from the 1920s to the present,
used their organizational position to craft a market niche for the
community college that differs from that of academically inclined
institutions. In opposition to four-year schools and universities,
committed to the arts and sciences, AACC officials sought to
identify the two-year college as a career-oriented alternative to
education aimed at preparing students for participation in public
life. In other words, for the sake of organizational interests, AACC
leaders worked to shape and reshape community colleges to meet
the changing needs of the marketplace, as opposed to preparing
students to meet the steady and timeless responsibilities placed on
citizens in a democracy.

Two-year colleges flourished under the influence of the AACC,
and the push to vocationalize the community college succeeded.
Still, there are consequences associated with the move toward occupational programs. Labaree suggests that AACC officials placed
personal and organizational objectives above broader social or
educational goals in the process of striving to create a market niche
for community colleges. In effect, whether the AACC intended to
or not, the group created a legacy that grips the institution like an
anchor. Labaree explains:

Seeking to preserve the vocational mission of the community college within the socially efficient division of education labor, public and private officials have generally been able to block its institutional mobility by denying it the right to award the bachelor's degree, thus freezing it in a permanently junior status within higher education. (1997, p. 213)

Labaree understands the effort to promote the schools' vocational role, from the standpoint of community colleges as organizations trying to establish a place for themselves in the higher education market; however, he suggests "that place is socially dysfunctional" (Labaree, 1997, p. 4). Community colleges succeeded in promoting their role as career-related training sites, but to the degree that colleges propagate vocational curricula, they create a scenario where the graduate of an associate degree or certificate program gains technical or professional training in a particular field of work, but is only incidentally, if at all, made ready for fulfilling the responsibilities of an adult American man, woman, parent, citizen or community leader (Labaree, 1997).

By comparison, undergraduate majors in the liberal arts do not necessarily earn their living in their chosen field. But the justification for majoring in math, English or history does not always reside in the idea that the major will be connected to a clear employment opportunity (Botstein, 1997). Undergraduate liberal arts majors find rewarding careers, but the motivation to immerse one's self in the liberal arts stems at least in part from the desire to become a steward of a discipline and an effective member of society. In contrast to the current focus on job training, public colleges were originally meant to serve a public purpose, the only purpose that could justify substantial public investment.

The Community College's Cultural Role

The conversation surrounding the community college baccalaureate is focused on economic concerns, although, the discussion could easily run parallel to the broad debate that took place over the nature of high school curricula in the early part of the last century. In the words of Carol Schneider, president of the American Association of Colleges and Universities, two groups with opposing views struggled to determine the character of high school education in the United States in the early 1900s, "One group of educators thought that all high school students ought to take a strong academic foundation in history, literature, science, mathematics, and language. But others—the progressives of the day!—thought the students who where were not college bound would be better served by less academic forms of learning" (2005, p. 63).

The outcome of the debate is clear today. "The proponents of a rigorous liberal education in the schools lost this battle," and as a result, "the public schools invented differential curriculum tracks" (Schneider, 2005, p. 63). There is an academic or college preparatory track for middle-class and upwardly mobile students, but there remains a vocational track for students with lower aptitudes or less familiarity with the arts and sciences. At the time the tracks were formed, as now, "The dividing lines were economic, with the affluent moving in one direction and the poor, including people of color and first generation families, moving in quite another" (Schneider, 2005, p. 63).

For more than a century, American conceptions of schooling have been tied to the notion of economic or social class mobility. However, the late Christopher Lasch suggested a careful look at historical records shows that, "The promise of American life came to be identified with social mobility only when more hopeful interpretations began to fade" (1995, p. 59). Lasch explains, "The concept of social mobility embodies a fairly recent and sadly impoverished understanding of the American Dream" (1995, p. 59). In *The Revolt of the Elites*, he draws attention to the idea that in recent U.S. history "money has come to be regarded as the only reliable measure of equality," but he notes, in the prior century, "Opportunity, as Americans understood it, was a matter more of intellectual than material enrichment" (1995, p. 59). In the past, the life of the mind added an element of equality to a society characterized by economic polarization. Today, by contrast, intellectual pursuits are unhinged from political culture, and educational institutions are conceived largely in terms of their contribution to state or regional economies.

Lasch stops short of turning his attention to contemporary high schools or community colleges, but scholars working in education confirm his point that it is the logic of cost-benefit analysis that structures our understanding of the purpose public institutions serve. "According to this logic, schools are producers of educational commodities—credentials—and must adapt themselves to meet the demands of the consumer" (Labaree, 1997, p. 4). In other words, institutional attention has been turned away from cultural goals and aimed instead at fulfilling private ambitions.

In the quest to cater curriculum and institutional mission to the demands of the marketplace, colleges and universities alike pursue narrow paths of specialization. Through the process of creating degree plans to match students' career interests, and the needs of employers to fill vacancies at each rank in their organizations, higher education institutions structured themselves on hierarchical lines, and as such we maintain a system marked by double standards. For the sons and daughters of the wealthy there are institutions committed to the civic arts and leadership. For the masses, we offer training in occupational fields. According to Lasch, this arrangement is not compatible with the goals of a democratic nation, where citizens are equally responsible for maintaining a vital public sphere. In his words, "Common standards are absolutely indispensable to a democratic society. Societies organized around a hierarchy of privilege can afford multiple standards, but democracies cannot" (Lasch, 1995, p. 88).

Those who stand opposed to the community college baccalaureate often express their opposition in the name of underprivileged students. Supporters of the two-year curriculum wish to keep the community college at the bottom of the postsecondary network, for fear that if baccalaureate programs expand, the community college might fail to serve students from low-income backgrounds.

Yet, the challenge is not to provide underprivileged students with an education of less value and of a different type than one finds at four-year institutions. The challenge is to provide those students with an education of the same nature that one finds at prestigious colleges and universities.

For the sake of compassion and concern for poor and minority students, those who wish to hold community colleges in their sub-baccalaureate status unwittingly press for the continuation of a pernicious double standard. Lasch is uncompromising on this point:

> When the ideology of compassion leads us to this type of absurdity, it is time to call it into question. Compassion has become the human face of contempt. Democracy once implied opposition to every form of double standard. Today we accept double standards—as always, a recipe for second class citizenship—in the name of humanitarian concern. (1995, p. 105)

The best means to address class-based inequality is not continued double standards in education. The best approach is egalitarianism. The baccalaureate is the standard postsecondary credential, and if large numbers of students are educated in sub-baccalaureate institutions, then the democratic ideal of equality is compromised.

Conclusion

As a mass of heretofore-excluded Americans entered postsecondary schools in the middle twentieth-century, higher education changed. When colleges and universities enrolled an exclusive group of elites, the curriculum focused on leadership and public service, but as women, minorities, and students of modest means won access to higher education, the focus on academics gave way to career-oriented programs. Whether the change came about through haplessness or cynical intentions, it is difficult to say.

With respect to community colleges, Dougherty argued the schools inadvertently became contradictory institutions when they moved away from academics and toward a mission centered on training in job-related fields (1994). Labaree concurs and suggests, "The community college seems to be caught in a bind that was constructed historically, as it sought to accomplish the contradictory aims of promoting political equality and market inequality within a single institution" (1997, p. 221). The bind Labaree describes should be the subject of debate among staff and faculty, but the goal of training workers to private sector criteria became so engrained in the culture of the community college during the past two decades, college professionals lost touch with the era when their institutions served the sole purpose of preparing students for success in a four-year course of study.

Ironically, the current move toward baccalaureate education holds the potential to stir demand and increase enrollment on the same line as the AACC had in mind when they sought to transform two-year schools into technical institutes. As colleges and universities sought to identify themselves as research-oriented institutions in the past half-century, a significant hole opened up in the higher education market. We currently lack a network of public four-year schools committed to teaching and undergraduate students. For the sake of organizational interests, community colleges will do well to fill this empty space in our postsecondary system. Instead of merely emulating university curriculum with the hope that higher status institutions will accept students' transfer credits, four-year community colleges free themselves to forge a new type of baccalaureate—tailored to the social and cultural needs of the communities that host our campuses.

The community college baccalaureate also affords us an occasion to discuss the role of education in society. But in order for the conversation to be genuine, it must involve voices other than those who would simply use public institutions to subsidize training costs sustained in the private sector; and the discussion must be conducted in terms other than that of economics. Decisions about the future of public education must be decided on educational grounds and with respect to public interests. The potential for the community college to contribute to American life is too crucial for the debate to be settled on the basis of economic goals alone.

Institutional mission, college-wide curriculum, and the teaching strategies that faculty use can and probably should focus on economics to some degree, but not for the purpose of producing trained and subordinate workers for regional businesses. The college classroom is one of the last places where citizens come together in public forums to talk about their shared futures and collective interests. To those ends, in the next chapter I outline the rationale and procedures for using the town hall meeting as a model for community college courses.

8

Pedagogy: The Town Hall Meeting as a Teaching Method

As a beginning community college instructor, I spent much of my time searching for a teaching method that would help create an engaged and critical classroom environment. I settled on a strategy that uses the New England town hall meeting as a model. In many ways, the town meeting represents an ideal forum for democracy, and it is a format well suited to the community college since the institution has long been considered "democracy's college." Theoretically, two-year schools were meant to democratize higher education, and in this chapter I propose a bridge from theory to practice. I offer the rationale and procedures for creating a classroom environment that rewards participation and supports democracy.

The Struggle to Encourage Democratic Teaching Methods

The learning college movement brought changes to the culture of two-year schools, and the changes came with repercussions that affect life in classrooms. With respect to teaching, the aspect of learning college culture with the most significant impact is the notion that educators, campuses and classrooms all impose unnecessary restrictions on the process of learning.

According to O'Banion, learning is time-bound, place-bound, and teacher-bound in traditional institutions (1997). The efforts of learning advocates have been aimed at overthrowing the time-honored physical and annual structure of education. The main objective is to free students from what they perceive to be constraints. Therefore, one of the primary goals of the learning college movement is to make coursework convenient—available anytime, anywhere, even at home or on the job.

In community colleges, the emphasis on providing education anytime and anywhere has meant a move to establish courses and degree programs on the Internet (Levin, 2002). The move toward distance education and electronic delivery came as good news to producers of educational software, as the learning college concept fits neatly with the technologically driven corporate training model favored in the private sector. American industries discovered long ago that employees can be trained online, alone, without an instructor or a public institution to host the endeavor. However, as two-year schools moved to aid industries with employee preparation, the new narrow focus on learning grew at odds with the broader and higher purpose of the two-year college: education.

In the rhetoric of the learning college movement, education is reduced to learning or cognitive development. Learning may be one of an educational institution's basic purposes, but at its foundation, the logic of the revolution rests on a conflation of learning with the larger process of becoming educated. Learning takes place everywhere, almost all of the time, but that cannot be said of education. For example, there is no question that you can learn by watching the Discovery Channel. But the question to ask is, "Can you become an educated person by watching the Discovery Channel?" For most, the answer is no you cannot.

What it means to be an educated person is something we debate, but there is agreement on the notion that education is a social institution. Education is an institution, just like the family, sports, religion, or the law. Like other institutions, education is complex. The facilitation of learning or cognitive development is part of the enterprise, but education is also a moral, cultural, and political process.

Recent technological innovations provide educators with new and exciting ways to promote student development, but an Internet-based curriculum in the community college is something worth careful consideration, with an eye toward the consequences. In particular, when technology breaks the bond between citizens and public institutions, we have reason to question our efforts at reform. In situations where electronic teaching methods sever the relationship between students and colleges, we have occasion to pause and consider the costs of our quest to alter education. In a strong democracy, public institutions do more than merely serve private interests. According to Robert Bellah and associates, public institutions such as community colleges "are the substantial forms through which we understand our own identity and the identity of others as we seek to achieve a decent society" (Bellah et al., 1991, p. 16).

There is a growing body of research demonstrating that students learn effectively, even when isolated from teachers and classmates (Merisotis and Phipps, 1999), but the process of becoming an educated person is lengthy and complicated. However it is defined, the process entails more than the acquisition of knowledge or skills. To be credentialed as an educated person means more than mere learning in the cognitive sense, it includes the development of purpose, integrity, and the fostering of an identity as an active member of a free republic (Chickering, 1969). Ideally, public education has a public purpose. Unfortunately, in the rush to reduce education to its most utilitarian role, the learning revolution undermined the lofty intent of two-year colleges.

The problem becomes more apparent when you consider social institutions outside of education in the same light currently used to view two-year schools. If one considers institutions like religion or even something as central to the American way of life as the neighborhood barbecue, in the terms currently used to describe colleges, the results are illuminating. For example, church services suffer some of the same drawbacks as classes. They are bound by time, place, and particular pastors or priests. Of course, it is possible to worship in the convenience of home, any time of the day or week. Therefore, one might ask, should Americans continue to take time out of their busy schedules to commune with others while they worship? Should we launch a revolution to dissuade the American people from attending churches? The easy answer is no, and the simple reason is that there is a lot more to being a member of a church than worship alone. Like education, religion is a social institution. Churches create a community where bonds are established, roles are enacted, norms are observed and values are shared.

The backyard barbecue serves as a similar example. Reduced to its most practical function, the purpose of a barbecue is to eat. As we know, the process of eating is not bound by time, place, or a particular cook. Should Americans continue to gather in backyards all over the country for the purpose of sharing meals, when everyone knows they can eat any time, on their own, and in private? The answer is yes. Americans should continue to gather for neighborhood barbecues because they are meaningful social and cultural occurrences. There can be no doubt that Americans attend outdoor barbecues in part to consume calories, but the institution is much more complicated than an analysis of its most practical purpose could suggest.

With examples like these, it is easy to see if we launched a revolution to reduce other institutions to their utilitarian functions, and labeled them as such—"worshiping churches" or "eating barbecues" for example—Americans would think it absurd. But in the community college there have been few questions raised in opposition to the "learning college" revolution. Over the course of the last two decades, faculty and staff have made Herculean efforts to ensure that community college education is convenient for students and amenable to industry, but convenience and vocational applicability have been won without reflection on what the changes mean for local communities, let alone American society.

Specific information about roles, norms, and values are rarely printed on official church service schedules, seldom seen on agendas for neighborhood barbecues, and almost never spelled out on college course syllabi. Even so, these are the very purposes the institutions serve. In fact, the purposes are so central to the maintenance of society they are woven into the fabric of daily life, invisible to all but the most thoughtful observers. It takes a reflective practitioner to uncover and give words to the processes most of us take part in each day but take for granted. Dennis McGrath and Martin Spear are two such practitioners. In a description of the processes at work in their own classrooms they suggest:

> Within classrooms faculty and students encounter and try to understand one another. They negotiate social norms, create forms of knowledge, modify their identities; they make meaning together. (1991, p. 5)

Even though these processes cannot be easily reduced to measurable learning outcomes, they are keys to the process of becoming educated. They are not described in college mission statements, and they do not appear on the lists of curricular objectives academic departments produce to satisfy accrediting agencies. Instead, they are part of every college's "hidden curriculum," the unspoken and often unrecognized processes that make education a rich, meaningful, contentious and rewarding institution (Jackson, 1968; Margolis, 2001).

It's Not What You Teach—It's How You Teach It

When I began teaching in the community college, I was still a graduate student finishing coursework of my own. For me the period was one of difficult transition. As I made the move away from my role as a student and toward my new role as a teacher, I was faced with a number of questions. How would I structure my courses? What kind of assignments would I require? What could I do to shape the tenor of the discussions I planned to hold in class? As I prepared to meet my first group of students, questions like these stretched out before me like a row of hurdles.

In my search for answers to the questions I faced as a teacher, I discovered the educational philosophy of John Dewey (1916, 1956). For Dewey, the development of a model teaching practice begins with an educator's image of an ideal society. For instance, if we wish to live in a society where people sit quietly and listen, schools requiring stillness and silence may be the shortest route to that end. On a similar note, if we wish to live in a society where people stay home and watch television, schools that use television as a vehicle for instruction should provide an avenue to that future. By contrast, if we wish to live in a society where citizens come together in public places to have meaningful conversations about the most compelling issues of the day, then schools must provide an environment where people can practice the art of citizenship, in a forum reminiscent of our most democratic institutions.

Years before the phrase had been coined, Dewey was attuned to the concept of the hidden curriculum (Dewey, 1916; Jackson, 1968). In short, he suggested the power of education lies as much in the social process of the classroom as it does in the subject matter outlined in a text or a set of class notes. As a graduate student, that was easy for me to understand. In one seminar after another, I could see and feel myself taking part in what were essentially exercises in socialization. Although I was expected to develop a working body of knowledge, I was also learning how to think and how to present ideas to others. I was developing a command of my subject, but I was also coming to know the protocol of public discourse.

I found the exchanges in my graduate seminars exciting, and as a faculty member I was eager to bring that same level of excitement to the classes I found myself teaching. Early on, I asked students to research a set of topics, and I required them to present their thoughts in class. I gave them a detailed set of instructions: I asked them to discuss their author's central argument, the appropriateness of the research methods, and the theoretical underpinnings of the work that they reviewed.

Despite careful planning on my part, the assignments flopped. On the rare occasion when a student took all of the steps prescribed in the project, I observed that it nearly always produced sighs and even occasional snickers from the class. When students used the terms of academic sociology, terms like "functionalist," or "symbolic interaction," it was evidently a sign of caving in to authority or "sucking up" to the instructor. At one point, I watched a student mouth the words "brown-noser" to a classmate under his breath as a fellow student described an author's theoretical framework.

Research on teaching in two-year schools confirmed that my experience was part of a broader pattern. Similar classroom dynamics are documented in the work of authors such as McGrath and Spear (1991), Shor (1980), and London (1978). McGrath and Spear suggest, in the community college:

> Students and teachers appear to disagree about the most basic, most mundane features of the classroom, as well as the larger vision of the nature and purpose of education. (1991, p. 5)

In an ethnographic account of life in a two-year college, London describes how tension can develop between teachers and students. He explains, "By stressing the value of intellectual activity...teachers became another reminder of what students thought to be their own shortcomings" (1977, p. 67). For this reason, Shor suggests, "students are suspicious of intellectuals" (1980, p. 29).

My attempts to draw students into an exchange prompted resistance, but for Shor, the solution to the question of how to overcome the suspicion and misgivings students bring to the classroom lies in the careful use of language. In his words, "the question is one of linguistic compatibility between teacher and students" (1980, p. 29). Subject matter aside, teachers and students are immersed in a ritual of culture—the college class. Terms of engagement are negotiated as part of the ritual, and social relations in a class unfold according to norms and roles that are mutually established by teachers and students. The norms and roles created and observed in a course form the foundation on which the learning of a subject takes place. They are central to the success of the undertaking, but they are hidden in the sense that they are not often discussed.

In my own practice I was experimenting, or fumbling as it were, with the hidden curriculum. In addition to passing on my discipline, I was working to create an environment that would allow students to observe and take part in a forum where public discourse was the norm, but I was struggling. The terms and values I brought with me from the university were a barrier to my success and the success of my students. Ethnographic accounts of the community college classroom confirmed my own observations—the language and concepts of the academy were stumbling blocks.

I started to look for a way to remove the jargon of social science from my conversations with students. Still faced with the question of how to structure my classes, I began experimenting with activities. I called them everything from "collective reviews" to "collegial discussions," but I met with little success. It was clear I needed a more colloquial title and a more prosaic format for the classroom environment I hoped to create.

Ironically, as a teacher, I was the one going through the process of socialization. The classroom ritual exerts a powerful force on both students and faculty—shaping and molding attitudes and actions. I was looking for a way to create an environment that would foster student behaviors that matched my expectations for rigor and participation, but ultimately my methods had to be delivered on my student's terms. Finally, I settled on the format of the New England town hall meeting. What method could be better suited to an institution described as democracy's college?

The Town Hall Meeting as a Teaching Method

As of this writing, I have been conducting town hall meetings in lower division courses for more than a decade. To start, I provide students with a general overview of the assignment, complete with a brief description of each stage involved. In the first phase of the activity, students determine the five to eight topics to be discussed in class. I allow them fifteen to twenty minutes to brainstorm a list of potential topics on Post-it notes in groups of four or five. When students have taken ample time to come up with ideas, I circulate among the groups, announce each topic to the class, and ask the others to remove duplicated topics from their lists. When we are through, we have one set of Post-it notes, with one distinct topic on each note.

Next, we assemble the notes on a table near the front of the room and I distribute three small adhesive dots to every student. I explain that each dot is a vote, and during the next stage of the activity every person casts three votes. Students vote by placing dots on the Post-it note(s) and topic(s) of their choice. In the end, I tally the number of dots per subject, and the top vote-winning issues are the ones that we discuss.

After topics are determined, typically the following class period, we hold a drawing to decide which town council each student will serve on and, in effect, which subjects they will study. The town councils are made up of four or five students, so I fill out four or five slips of paper for each topic. On each slip of paper, there is an issue and a date. Once I assemble enough slips of paper for each topic, they all go into a hat (I keep a hat, locally known as the Sombrero of Destiny, in my office for this purpose). I bring the hat to class, and from it students choose their topics and the date of the meeting where they serve on the town council. This element of serendipity gives students incentive to take the selection of topics seriously. They know in advance that they may be required to research any one of the top vote-winning issues.

When we have a council committed to each subject, I provide students with a form on which to record their research activities. Students are required to bring a minimum of two sources to the table when it comes time for them to share their work in class. The form contains space for bibliographic information on each source, along with three questions I expect students to answer during the meetings. I ask them to think about whether their authors' perspectives are biased. I also ask them to think about the data presented and whether it is valid or reliable, and I encourage them to reflect on their reading and preparation. In the end, I make a point to ask students about their original positions. I ask them to talk about whether their research either confirmed or challenged their prior convictions.

In addition to completing the form that I provide, students are also required to prepare a set of talking points. Ground rules for the discussion require students to prepare a set of notes for their part on the town council, but the rules also specify that their part cannot be so detailed that it reads like a script. I show students three or four examples of talking points in class, prepared on a range of different subjects, and from there, students are free to use the format that suits their interests and their articles.

As for the meetings themselves, I ask council members to sit as part of a panel in the front of the classroom. We determine an order or progression prior to the start, with a logical beginning, middle, and end. Once the council begins sharing information, the remaining students are free to ask questions or make comments. In fact, students are required to participate in the meetings. They earn two points per meeting by either making comments or raising questions. In the past, I asked students to mark their participation by placing Post-it notes on their desks (Hanson, 2000). Today, I allow students to keep track of their own participation on the honor system. They fill out a checklist I provide them at the beginning of the semester. Over the course of the past decade, I have had considerable success with this method and very little incidence of fraud. With few exceptions, students have been forthright when keeping a record of their contributions.

Assessment

As evidenced in an evaluation survey I conducted for three consecutive semesters, students appear to be comfortable with the town hall format. It seems the meetings afford them opportunities to think and grow. From an educational standpoint, students affirm that in-class town meetings challenge them to think critically and creatively. Students also claim the activity helps build their capacity to analyze research. In large part, I suspect that is true since the assignment requires them to study a subject in some depth. In addition, from a social and political point of view, the meetings

Table 8.1
Student Perceptions of Town Hall Meetings

Town Hall Meetings:	Mean	Percent "Agree" or "Strongly Agree"	N of Evaluation
…were a good way for me to participate in class discussions.	4.40	94.00	124
…helped me learn how to analyze research.	4.07	84.00	124
…were a chance to listen to a wide range of views.	4.48	95.00	125
…were a good opportunity to practice public speaking in a comfortable setting.	4.28	90.40	125
…allowed me to see the political side of social problems.	4.16	90.40	125
…encouraged me to think creatively about current events.	4.24	90.40	125
…encouraged me to think critically about current events.	4.27	91.13	124
…were a good way to study a subject in depth.	4.23	87.90	124

Note: Perceptions range from 1 = "strongly disagree" to 5 = "strongly agree."

provide a comfortable forum for students to practice participation in a public sphere, both as speakers and listeners.

One shortcoming of the evaluation research I have conducted to date is that it is based on an attitudinal survey as opposed to a direct measure of student performance. Even so, from the data I collected I am comfortable concluding that students enjoy the meetings. I am also confident that their reports of learning were given in earnest.

In my own discipline, sociology, the town hall forum lends itself to the subject matter, but the format could easily be adapted for use in other fields. For example, nursing instructors could use the format to provide students with an opportunity to discuss current healthcare issues. English teachers could use the activity to structure dialogues on the use of language in politics, advertising, or the media. Biology faculty could conduct town hall meetings on topics such as endangered species or invasive, non-native plants. Anywhere they are practiced, town meetings stand to make good on the promise of democracy's college. The technique mirrors the structure and social relations found in the most democratic of our institutions.

Conclusion

The learning revolution and learning college culture made it difficult for teachers to challenge the conceit that education is a business, learning is a product, and measurable outcomes are more valuable than the quality of the process by which students are educated. The debates over the social role of two-year schools and the best means to embody the spirit of democracy's college seem over, at least for the moment.

But in retrospect, the historic debate over the role and mission of the community college never had much to do with democracy. Critics of the community college were concerned that two-year schools lacked the potential to create upward economic mobility for the American working class (Zwerling, 1976). Generally speaking, advocates of the two-year school acknowledged the colleges could not ensure class mobility, but they maintained that the schools provide avenues for individual success (Cohen and Brawer, 1987). Even in the age when scholars had the courage to question the role of two-year colleges, the debate focused on the question of whether or not the institutions could build a more prosperous society. Despite all of the rhetoric about the democratization of higher education, and even despite the title—democracy's college—scholars have yet to consider the role of the community college in the creation and maintenance of a strong democracy.

In Ernest Pascarella and Patrick Terenzini's classic, *How College Affects Students*, the authors reviewed more than 2,600 research projects aimed at understanding the social, economic, political, moral and psychological impact of postsecondary education (1991). They only uncovered one study of political engagement and social responsibility among two-year college students, and it was unpublished (Marks, 1990). The study suggested "two-year college attendance is negatively related to changes in social responsibility" (Pascarella and Terenzini, 1991, p. 300).

Apart from research aimed specifically at two-year schools, the most comprehensive source of data on undergraduate student norms is the annual Freshman National Norms survey conducted by the staff of the Higher Education Research Institute (HERI) at the University of California, Los Angeles. Reporting on the 2001 survey for the *Chronicle of Higher Education*, Alex Kellog notes, "political engagement among college freshman has reached an all-time low...only 28 percent of entering college students reported an interest in keeping up to date with political affairs, the lowest level since the survey was established in 1966" (2001, p. A47). By the fall of 2007, the proportion rose to 37.2 percent (Sax, Astin, Lindholm, Korn, Saenz, and Mahoney, 2007). The rise is noteworthy, but the figures are still too low for those that view public education as preparation for public life.

Prior to the year 2000, community college students were included as part of the sample in the HERI study of Freshman National Norms. Unfortunately, beginning at the turn of the century, students attending two-year colleges were no longer surveyed. According to Vivian Deluna, HERI staff member, "The number of two-year colleges participating dropped gradually since the late 1980s with an increasing turnover in the two-year colleges that participate." The authors of the annual report explain:

> The combination of these factors has resulted in ever-larger cell weights being applied to the two-year college data and increased the possibility of non-random variation in the overall national norms (Sax, Astin, Korn and Mahoney, 2000, p. 113).

The absence of two-year college students from the Freshman National Norms survey is an unfortunate development, but prior data suggests, had two-year college students been included, their level of interest in politics would have fallen short of the national average. In 1999, the last year community college students were included in the study, 20.7 percent of two-year college freshmen considered keeping up to date with political affairs important or very important; hardly a glowing endorsement for an institution described as democracy's college (Sax, Astin, Horn, and Mahoney, 1999).

To address political apathy on two-year college campuses, educators are going to have to take a more direct approach to fostering the quality of mind that makes effective citizens. As a teaching method, town hall meetings are a start. They are a means to reassert the community college's social and political roles—roles that have been under attack for more than two decades.

The current learning revolution notwithstanding, even in the early eighties there were signs that community colleges were being transformed into tax-supported training sites for multinational companies. In their work on the history of two-year schools, Cohen and Brawer (1987) offered an early eulogy for the community college's broader role in society, and a preview of the current emphasis on what they consider the college's main purpose—workforce development:

Each time the colleges act as social welfare agencies or modern Chautauquas, they run the risk of reducing the support they must have if they are to pursue their main purpose. (1982, p. 282)

The data I collected as part of my search for a promising class-room structure suggest it is time for community college profession-als to start taking the risks Cohen and Brawer cautioned us against. By the turn of the century, capitalism had demonstrated itself to be global in its scope and influence. But at the same time, it is has also been argued that democracy stands "on trial" (Elshtain, 1993). The free enterprise system gains new devotees every day around the globe, while American democracy withers on the vine, strangled by low voter turnout and a less than well-informed electorate.

It is time for those who call democracy's college their profes-sional home to start taking democracy seriously. As public servants, community college teachers have an obligation to confront the shifting mission of the two-year school toward serving global eco-nomic interests at the expense of the institution's role in the affairs of their host communities. As educators, two-year college teach-ers also have a responsibility to counter the trend toward political disengagement among students. As a teaching method, town hall meetings hold the promise of addressing both concerns.

Epilogue:
The Twenty-First-Century College

The community college is a twentieth-century institution. The growth and expansion of the two-year school in the era that followed the Second World War is unrivaled in scope. The number of public community colleges tripled in the two decades that mark the postwar period. A cultural and demographic tide drove the expansion. Civic-minded advocates pushed for increased access to education, and heretofore-marginalized groups demanded greater opportunities. In response, states built postsecondary networks aimed at improving the nation's quality of life. Legislatures acted with the intent to increase educational parity, while at the same time enlisting talents that were formerly unrecognized.

The seeds of equality and inclusiveness sewn in the postwar period went dormant in the political climate of the 1980s, however. Conservative ideology guided the thoughts and actions of global leaders during the decade of the eighties. Individualism reigned, public institutions saw their budgets cut by sizable proportions, and ultimately England's Prime Minister, Margaret Thatcher declared, "There is no such thing as society" (1987, p. 10). In retrospect, the declaration sounds absurd, but the claim served to wrest attention and legitimacy from public institutions dedicated to the common good—institutions such as schools, colleges, labor unions, welfare agencies, and environmental organizations. British and American conservatives both saw such entities as a threat to the potential for businesses to pursue their interests, unfettered by criticisms or regulations.

In a break with the sentiments of the Theodore Roosevelt and Dwight D. Eisenhower administrations, Reagan-era conservatives fought the idea that public nonprofit organizations serve as a counter-balance to the self-interests of entrepreneurs. They worked to turn nonprofit organizations away from the goal of challenging commercial values and the beliefs endemic to market ideology. In particular, Reagan-era leaders sought to reorder public schools, such that they shaped their practices to match the needs of businesses.

In accord with the political culture of the late twentieth century, community college staff and faculty also began moving toward a curriculum meant to fulfill the institution's self-interests. But according to William Sullivan, colleges changed their mission and purpose "at the expense of both long-term democratic values and the academy's contribution to society's self-reflective capacity" (1997, p. 4). Two-year schools abandoned their potential to serve as a public forum or sphere from which to generate a critique of social or cultural conditions. Community colleges were not the only schools to undergo such a shift, however.

The authors of the 2003 volume *Educating Citizens* describe a wholesale transformation of American higher education, beginning in the middle 1900s. The change involved a drift away from character development and toward a greater emphasis on "practical and vocational education, scientific instruction and investigation" (Colby, Ehrlich, Beaumont, and Stevens, 2003, p. 28). There is a consensus among historians that the move was driven by an attempt to reconfigure American higher education along lines that matched the model of the German university.

The shift away from the British collegiate ideal and toward a German focus on research inspired a debate among scholars and educators. Knefelkamp and Schneider explain, "Those who wanted the academy involved in the work of building a moral democracy came into conflict with the view that the academy should devote itself to the production of knowledge;" but they also suggest, "proponents of the research agenda were better organized," and they conclude by acknowledging that, "the struggle was a rout" (1997, p. 330). American institutions adopted the German emphasis on scientific advancement as opposed to education or character formation, and as public colleges expanded to become universities, they also began to adopt the German model stressing the value of research.

Two-year colleges evolved along similar lines. Although they did not include the production of new knowledge as part of their mission, community colleges shifted their attention away from the liberal arts and placed their focus on industry-specific programs (Levin, 2001). With respect to the changes two-year colleges underwent, Cohen and Brawer suggest, "The old values of liberal education became supplemental—adjuncts to be picked up incidentally, if at all, along the way to higher paying employment" (1987, p. 20). Thus, with the founding notion that colleges contribute to the maintenance of a civil society brushed aside and minimized, two-year schools began to conduct themselves in a fashion consistent with a philosophy of "instrumental individualism" (Sullivan, 1997, p. 2). Community colleges quietly moved away from a liberal arts curriculum meant to pass on culture and instill habits of mind and toward training programs with the intent to serve the immediate interests of students and prospective employers.

In addition to the shifts in mission and curriculum, student attitudes also changed in the latter part of the twentieth century. The number of U.S. freshman entering higher education with the intent to "develop a meaningful philosophy of life" declined from 1967 to 2003, while those conceiving postsecondary schools as a means to becoming "well-off financially" increased (Sax, Astin, Lindholm, Korn, Saenz, and Mahoney, 2003, p. 7). Unfortunately, in the context of changing undergraduate views, colleges simply responded by structuring curricula to meet students' demands, as opposed to helping them explore the deeper meaning of their own norms, roles or values. As a consequence, students began to conceive higher education as a financial investment.

In the past, college teachers saw it as their duty to cast a critical eye on social and political patterns. Faculty assumed they held a responsibility to "raise questions that society does not want to ask" (Shapiro, 2005, p. 4) but in the last thirty years, and in community colleges specifically, the emphasis shifted toward offering technical degrees and short-term certificates in areas that appear in high demand.

Of course, colleges evolve. Organizations that rely on public financial support cannot afford to risk irrelevance, but public institutions are responsible for more than responding to the demands of the marketplace. In democracies, the role of higher education matches that of a free press. Historically, college faculty analyzed and evaluated emerging trends and events in society, and they did so under the assumption that they fulfilled their roles by accepting the responsibility to influence social life in the name of the common good, as opposed to simply serving fiscal interests. Sullivan explains:

> Like journalism, higher education is in the business of shaping its public as well as responding to it. Both institutions play crucial roles in making democratic societies viable: their activities are critical if public deliberation is to work at all under modern conditions. The way journalism and higher education conceive and carry out their purposes—the way they understand themselves—is integral to their ability to function as responsible institutions. (1997, p. 6)

Faculty willing to serve as social critics are as indispensable to a free society as an independent press. Like journalists, faculty are obliged to speak, write, and teach along moral lines, whether or not those lines coincide with the interests of wealth and power. Colleges have a role to play with respect to preparing students for careers, but their real influence lies in the ability to shape expectations about "what skills and knowledge are valuable, what career aspirations are reasonable and admirable, what kind of society Americans want to have, and what kind of people they want to be" (Sullivan, 1997, p. 12). In other words, colleges have a duty to create forums where students give thought to the question of what it means to live a good life, as opposed to simply making a living.

In the past, students used to come to colleges prepared for immersion into academic disciplines, but today they come with expectations about their futures in the marketplace. Even so, in the current climate faculty can encourage students to see that their preparation for a career is only complete when it includes an understanding of the larger "social and intellectual context that gives work deeper meaning" (Colby, Ehrlich, Beaumont, and Stevens, 2003, p. 40). The sciences and humanities provide a frame of reference from which individuals can gauge their own prospects and assess their success in the pursuit of a life well lived. The liberal arts provide a foundation upon which people strive in relation to the prominent figures in human history, and in the process talents are realized, creativity is unlocked, and potential is brought to bear on problems of importance to the nation and the world.

Given the community college's size and prevalence, it is not an overstatement to suggest that the overall health of the society depends on the willingness and ability of staff and faculty to change the institution's course. If community colleges are to become exponents of critical thought and democratic participation, it is going to require an honest assessment of our current organizations. Prior to the turn of the century, McGrath and Spear offered hope and advice:

> Community colleges may yet, with energy and ingenuity, form themselves into powerful instruments for social equity … may yet offer poor, minority, and other nontraditional students an education of substance and quality. For that to happen, however, community college faculty and administrators must learn to be more self-critical and reflective about their institutions. (1991, p.7)

Advanced capitalist societies produce demands for countless services, and to perform those services employees need specialized training. Most educators understand the demand for electronic technicians, auto body repair people, and metal workers of various kinds. But to acknowledge the economic demand for narrowly-trained employees is to state the obvious, and in the process of routinely stating the obvious, community college staff and faculty forgot that the United States is more than an economy. We allowed ourselves to forget that public colleges serve the purpose of educating citizens—responsible for maintaining our social life and civic culture. There is no reason why community colleges should not offer specialized courses, but there is also ample reason to suggest that those courses should be offered during the third and fourth years of bachelor's degrees.

Employers are rarely interested in ensuring that workers operate with a sense of autonomy and independence, such that they are willing to challenge the authority of superiors. In contrast, citizens in a democracy must maintain a sense of self-determination strong enough to assure a willingness to challenge or replace local, state, and federal officials. Unlike hierarchical organizations in the business world, democratic societies place an identical set of demands on each adult member of the population.

Economically viable skills can be developed in a broad range of settings; abilities of interest to employers can be learned and practiced at home or on the job, but what of the traits and characteristics associated with strong and active citizens? If community colleges do not work to incite a spirit of inquiry and activism, then who will? Higher education institutions are one of the last remnants of physical space for critical dialogue within our shrinking public sphere. If community colleges devote themselves to labor force development or students' financial interests, then we fail to make good on the promise of a liberally educated populace.

Community colleges hold the potential to help realize Thomas Jefferson's dream of a nation characterized by political participation and widespread equality, although, such a purpose is not likely to evolve on its own, without effort. Institutional commitment to nonmarket values and liberal education waned in the past three decades, and through the process of organizational socialization, faculty learned to accept market values and workforce development goals in their place. Teachers and staff committed to the liberal arts face a challenge when it comes to making their work a priority in the present day community college.

Yet, a renewed commitment to liberal or general education holds more than just the promise of changing student's lives or restoring the community college's social and political roles. The change also comes with potential organizational benefits. A move away from narrow job-related training and toward general education stands to make two-year schools more competitive in the postsecondary marketplace. In addition, by moving the focus of our efforts from training to education, we equip colleges to fulfill their responsibilities as public institutions, and we position our schools to make sound investments with tax dollars.

The Liberal Arts Are Competitive in the Marketplace

The postsecondary marketplace is competitive. Generally speaking, local, state, and federal higher education budgets shrank from coast to coast throughout the 1990s, and the trend continues here in the first part of the new century (Rouche and Jones, Eds., 2005). In addition to budget shortfalls, public two-year colleges were also forced to compete with a host of new institutions geared toward serving private sector interests (Boggs, 2005). In response to the competition, community colleges began changing their public image to match that of the growing number of for-profit training institutes. In effect, over the course of the last decade, community colleges worked to become more like their competitors.

According to Richard Alfred, "Most institutions focus on keeping pace with rivals and, as a result, their marketing strategies tend to converge" (2000, p. 14). In the case of community colleges, the strategy hinged on the notion that two-year schools should become convenient places for students to acquire labor market skills. Higginbottom and Romano suggest, "Community colleges see themselves as the workforce training centers of the 21st century," and they go on to explain, "Increasingly this is taken to mean short-term training of job-related skills, as opposed to the broader goals of general education" (2001, p. 255). Through the process of identifying themselves as vocational centers, public two-year schools shifted their missions (Ayers, 2005) and organizational culture (Levin, 2001) to match the norms and values found in the private sector; Nordstrom's department store is even used as an organizational model (Pickelman, 2005).

Through the course of trying to emulate competitors, two-year schools turned attention away from the practice of "establishing a *brand identity* that distinguishes it in the eyes of customers" (Alfred, 2000, p. 14). Instead of striving to establish a proud and unique public image, community colleges refashioned themselves as job-training institutes; a distinction that does little to inspire respect or reverence in the minds of students.

Like it or not, the nation's postsecondary system is structured hierarchically. Status and prestige are intertwined with cost, selectivity, and purpose (Alfred and Horowitz, 1990). I suspect that many of us hope for a future where the arrangement is more egalitarian, but there can be no question that Ivy League schools are perched at the top, comprehensive state universities occupy the middle rungs, and community colleges fall somewhere near the bottom of the ladder. Potential students are conscious of the status differences, and economic models suggest that when it is possible, consumers choose the highest level of prestige at the lowest price (Breneman, 1996). In the words of Lyall and Sell, "As students become customers, they become more price sensitive, brand-name aware, and quality oriented. These factors, which have been at play in the private university sector for some time, are gaining importance in public higher education as well" (2006, p. 51). The same authors go on to note that, "The 'public-ivy' universities now generate far more demand than they have capacity to satisfy," and public community colleges have the ability to generate similar levels of demand (2006, p. 51).

As part of the process of securing their position in the marketplace, institutions of all types work to create an image that appeals to potential students, and for pragmatic reasons, that identity or image should be set as high on the status hierarchy as possible.

Students predisposed toward lower rungs on the ladder are likely to be motivated by a chance at high status, without an associated rise in costs. Similarly, prospective students inclined toward the middle may be drawn to the low cost of community colleges, if the choice could be made without a corresponding loss of prestige. By contrast, those same students, leaning toward the middle, are likely to steer away from schools lowering themselves to the bottom of the hierarchy by making vocational training the central feature of their enterprise.

Community colleges have everything to gain by becoming more like institutions in the middle or at the top of the postsecondary ladder, and the move is well within our grasp, as public two-year schools are endowed with assets online for-profit colleges can only dream about—campuses and full-time faculty. Community colleges are premier public places, where citizens from across a locality can join together for the purpose of higher education. When these strengths and advantages are explained to stakeholders and constituents, the results are palpable. For example, students at Piedmont Community College in Charlotte, North Carolina describe the school in the following terms, "It is a real academic institution. It has a beautiful campus. Classes are small and instructors really care" (Alfred, 2000, p. 18). Two-year colleges have more in common with high-status institutions than they have with private training organizations with no commitment to public service. Thus, community colleges are in a unique position to use the prestige and purpose of the liberal arts to strengthen their foothold in the marketplace.

The Liberal Arts Are Public

Public two-year schools are heavily subsidized. Community college students pay a fraction of the cost of their education in the form of tuition. The bulk of their education is subsidized by local, state, and federal taxpayers (Romano, 2003). Still, students conceive themselves as customers and colleges relate to them as such. Of course, within our culture it is routine to approach students from the standpoint of customer-service, but public colleges enter an unbefitting realm when they use prospective students' private and personal interests as a foundation for marketing strategies, and as of late, community colleges have worked to create public images designed to appeal to students' monetary interests.

The fundamental mission of public two-year schools is to serve the social and cultural needs of the communities of which they are a part, but in the past thirty years two-year colleges moved to make their goals synonymous with those of multinational companies. In this regard, two-year colleges and universities underwent similar changes. According to Frank Newman, director of the Futures Project at Brown University, institutions of all types have allowed their goals to be determined by economic forces, and he suggests the focus on economic development holds the potential to undermine public confidence and, therefore, public support for education. He writes:

> Over their long history, universities and colleges—both state-owned and private—have held a privileged position because of their focus on the needs of society rather than on self gain. With that position have come certain responsibilities. But today, as higher education becomes more closely linked to for-profit activities and market forces, its special status is endangered. (2000, p. 17)

In short, we are moving toward a point where, "education could be considered a private indulgence that, whatever its value to an individual, does not deserve public support" (Shapiro, 2005, p. 90).

More so than other institutions, community colleges depend on public financing. The best way to ensure the continued availability of public funds for two-year schools is to emphasize the social and public nature of our work. The message has to be clear—community colleges prepare students to "take on the full responsibilities of citizenship" (Labaree, 1997, p. 42). Two-year schools do not exist to merely subsidize the training costs of corporations; they exist to ensure that citizens have the capacity to act as full participants in our American democracy.

Community college curricula and advertising currently focus on appealing to students' self-interest and their desire for convenient access to credentials, but this move is out of step with the mission of a public institution. In the near term, students may have an interest in the fastest and most convenient route to becoming certified as members of a profession, but if we oblige them by offering mere convenience, we do students a disservice, and we also fail to live up to our own obligations.

Colleges have different goals than the armed forces, but they are both institutions with a commitment to public service. Therefore, colleges could learn from the example set by the military, with respect to their approach to new recruits. In the case of the Air Force, the historical call was to, "Aim high." The Army issued a challenge to, "Be all you can be," and the Navy currently implores recruits to "accelerate their lives." These institutions challenge prospective service people to use their individual abilities to serve a higher purpose. As institutions, the Army, Navy, and Air Force serve as reminders that selflessness and social responsibility are necessary to the health and maintenance of a free and democratic nation.

Community colleges could serve as a similar reminder. However, if we emphasize self-interest and convenience in our efforts, we avoid the expectations placed on us as institutions, and we also deprive students of the self-respect that accompanies hard work, commitment, and sacrifice. When graduates reflect on their community college experience, they are entitled to better and more meaningful memories than, "That was convenient."

There is no question that contemporary students approach prospective colleges from the standpoint of asking, "What can this school do for me?" (Labaree, 1997, p. 51). But community colleges have an obligation to teach students there is a more important question to ask, "What can this college help me do for my community?"

Conclusion

Over the course of the past thirty years, community colleges worked to circumvent their liberal arts curriculum. They did so by emphasizing applied associate degrees, and short-term certificates that contain little or no general education. In the process, we became invested in a pattern that President George W. Bush described as a form of "soft bigotry" that derives from having low expectations for students. By limiting our focus to job training, community colleges engage in a pattern of relating to students as if they were purely one-dimensional; as if economically valuable cognitive skills are the only traits they are competent to possess. Students are increasingly thought of and described as "workers" in the community college, and in the process, their lives as citizens and members of communities are systematically neglected.

Community colleges serve historically disadvantaged groups: women, minorities, people of low socio-economic status, and first generation college students (Adelman, 2005). As professionals, our challenge is to provide those students with an education of the same nature and character that one finds at the top levels of our postsecondary network. To offer community college students anything less is to partake in a subtle, but socially consequential form of bigotry. Unfortunately, when we limit the scope of our efforts to simply training employees, we deny our students the broad education for citizenship that takes place at the upper levels of the postsecondary hierarchy.

The most effective way to widen the narrow and limiting approach to education ushered in by occupationalism is to change the paradigm that shapes our thoughts and actions. In the decade of the 1990s, and here in the first part of the new century, community colleges gave in to market forces and aligned themselves with private sector interests. The change in mission and culture that accompanied the shift caused us to neglect our social identity. For the sake of our students and the nation, the time is right for a change in the norms and practices of faculty and staff.

As community colleges make the shift toward offering bachelor's degrees, it is reasonable to assume that upper-division coursework in a major will focus on immersion in a discipline or specialization. But until community colleges become baccalaureate-granting schools, the only course of action with integrity is to restore the liberal arts to a central place in the curriculum, so the efforts of college employees are consistent with the institution's proud historic goals.

Thomas Jefferson envisioned a public education network built to bestow citizens, even those of modest means, with a sense of competence so they do not back down in discussions with the wealthy or the powerful. Jefferson hoped to endow Americans from all walks of life with the ability to hold their heads high and know that their propensity to reason is uniquely their own and independent from anything that the affluent are able to buy or otherwise control. An educational system with such a capacity stood at the center of Jefferson's dream for the new nation, and for those that work in community colleges, the fulfillment of Jefferson's dream is a daily opportunity.

References

Adelman, C. (1992). *The Way We Are: The Community College as American Thermometer*. Washington, D.C.: U.S. Department of Education.

Adelman, C. (2005). *Moving into Town—And Moving On: The Community College in the Lives of Traditional-age Students*. Washington, D.C.: U.S. Department of Education.

Aldrich, H. and Pfeffer, J. (1976). Environments of Organizations. *Annual Review of Sociology,* (2), 79-105.

Alfonso, M., Bailey, T. and Scott, M. (2004). The Educational Outcomes of Sub-Baccalaureate Students: Evidence from the 1990s. *Economics of Education Review, 24*(2), 197-212.

Alfred, R. (2000). Assessment as a Strategic Weapon. *Community College Journal, 70*(4), 12-18.

Alfred, R. and Horowitz, M. (1990). Higher Education and Public Perception: Dynamics of Institutional Stature. *Journal for Higher Education Management, 6*(1), 7-28.

Apple, M. (1986). *Teachers and Texts: A Political Economy of Class and Gender Relations in Education*. New York: Routledge.

Apple, M. and Jungck, S. (1992). You Don't Have to be a Teacher to Teach this Unit: Teaching, Technology, and Control in the Classroom. Pp. 20-42 in *Understanding Teacher Development*. Edited by A. Hargraves and M. Fullan. New York: Teacher's College Press.

Ayers, D. (2005). Neoliberal Ideology in Community College Mission Statements: A Critical Discourse Analysis. *The Review of Higher Education, 28*(4), 527-49.

Barber, B. (1992). *An Aristocracy for Everyone: The Politics of Education and the Future of America*. New York: Oxford University Press.

Barkan, S. (2004). *Criminology: A Sociological Understanding*. Upper Saddle River, NJ: Prentice-Hall.

Barnett, R. (1994). *The Limits of Competence: Knowledge, Higher Education and Society.* Buckingham, UK: Society for Research into Higher Education and the Open University Press.

Barnett, R. (2003). *Beyond All Reason: Living with Ideology in the University.* Buckingham, UK: Society for Research into Higher Education and the Open University Press.

Barr, R. and Tagg, J. (1995). From Teaching to Learning—A New Paradigm for Undergraduate Education. *Change, 27*(6), 12-25.

Bates, R. (1992). Barely Competent: Against the Deskilling of the Professions via the Cult of Competence. Paper presented at the Seminar on Competency and Professional Education, University of Canberra. September, 1992.

Baum, L. F. (1983). Preface. Pp. ix-xvi in *The Wizard of Oz: The Critical Heritage Series*, Edited by M. P. Hearn. New York: Shocken Books.

Bean, J. (1998). Alternative Models of Professorial Roles: New Language to Reimagine Faculty Work. *The Journal of Higher Education, 69*(5), 496-512.

Beers, C. (2000). It's a Gas. *Wyoming Wildlife, 64*(6), 22-29.

Bellah, R., Madsen, R., Sullivan, W., Swidler, A., and Tipton, S. (1985). *Habits of the Heart: Individualism and Commitment in American Life.* Berkeley, CA: University of California Press.

Bellah, R., Madsen, R., Sullivan, W., Swidler, A., and Tipton, S. (1991). *The Good Society.* New York: Vintage Books.

Bishop, B. and Cushing, R. (2008). *The Big Sort.* New York: Houghton Mifflin.

Blair, D., Phinney, L. and Phillipe, K. (2001). International Programs at Community Colleges. *AACC Research Brief.* Washington D.C.: American Association of Community Colleges.

Blocker, C., Plummer, R. and Richardson, R. (1965). *The Two-Year College: A Social Synthesis.* Englewood Cliffs, NJ: Prentice-Hall.

Boggs, G. (1995). The Learning Paradigm. *Community College Journal, 66*(3), 24-27.

Boggs, G. (2005). Foreward. Pp. v in *The Entrepreneurial Community College.* Edited by J. Roueche and B. Jones. Washington, D.C: American Association of Community Colleges.

Botstein, L. (1997). *Jefferson's Children: Education and the Promise of American Culture.* New York: Doubleday.

Bourdieu, P. and Passeron, J.C. (1977). *Reproduction in Education, Society, and Culture.* London: Sage Publications.

Bowen, H. (1977). *Investment in Learning: The Individual and Social Value of Higher Education.* San Francisco: Jossey-Bass.

Bowles, S. and Gintis, H. (1976). *Schooling in Capitalist America: Educational Reform and the Contradictions of Economic Life.* New York: Basic Books.

Bragg, D. (2001). Opportunities and Challenges for the New Vocationalism. Pp. 5-16 in *The New Vocationalism in Community Colleges.* Edited by D. Bragg. New Directions for Community Colleges No. 115. San Francisco: Jossey Bass.

Braverman, H. (1974). *Labor and Monopoly Capital: The Degradation of Work in the Twentieth Century.* New York: Monthly Review Press.

Breneman, D. (1996). Affordability and the Private Institution. *Educational Record, 77*(4), 14, 17.

Brick, M. (1964). *Forum and Focus for the Junior College Movement: The American Association of Community Colleges.* New York: Teachers College Press.

Brint, S. and Karabel, J. (1989). *The Diverted Dream: Community Colleges and the Promise of Educational Opportunity in America, 1900-1985.* New York: Oxford University Press.

Brint, S. (2003). Few Remaining Dreams: Community Colleges Since 1985. *The Annals of the American Academy of Political and Social Science, 1*(586), 16-37.

Burns, J. M. (1965). *Presidential Government: The Crucible of Leadership.* Boston: Houghton-Mifflin.

Burris, B. and Heydebrand, W. (1984). Technocratic Administration and Educational Control. Pp. 236-255 in *Critical Studies in Organization and Bureaucracy.* Edited by F. Fischer and C. Sirianni. Philadelphia: Temple University Press.

Carnoy, M. and Levin, H. (1985). *Schooling and Work in the Democratic State.* Palo Alto, CA: Stanford University Press.

Carnevale, A. (2008). College for all? *Change, 40*(1), 23-29.

Center for Workforce Preparation and the American Association of Community Colleges (2003a). *Building Market Driven Systems: A National Dialogue.* Transcripts of Regional Dialogue, July 16, 2003. Schnecksville, PA.

Center for Workforce Preparation and the American Association of Community Colleges (2003b). *Building Market Driven Systems: A National Dialogue.* Transcripts of Regional Dialogue, September 30, 2003. Chicago, IL.

Center for Workforce Preparation and the American Association of Community Colleges (2003c). *Building Market Driven Systems: A National Dialogue.* Transcripts of Regional Dialogue, November 13, 2003. Seattle, WA.

Center for Workforce Preparation and the American Association of Community Colleges (2004). *Building Market Driven Systems: A National Dialogue.* Transcripts of Regional Dialogue, January 27, 2004. New Orleans, LA.

Chickering, A. (1969). *Education and Identity.* San Francisco: Jossey-Bass.

Ciccarelli, S. and Meyer, G. (2005). *Psychology* 2nd Edition. Upper Saddle River, NJ: Prentice-Hall.

Clark, B. (1980). The Cooling Out Function Revisited. *New Directions for Community Colleges, 8*(4), 15-32.

Clark, B. (1960). The Cooling Out Function in Higher Education. *The American Journal of Sociology, 65*(6), 569-576.

Cohen, A. and Brawer, F. (1987). *The American Community College.* San Francisco: Jossey-Bass.

Colby, A., Erlich, T., Beaumont, E. and Stevens, J. (2003). *Educating Citizens: Preparing America's Undergraduates for Lives of Moral and Civic Responsibility.* San Francisco: Jossey-Bass.

Conant, J. B. (1963). *Thomas Jefferson and the Development of American Public Education*. Berkley, CA: University of California Press.

Deiner, T. (1986). *Growth of an American Invention: A Documentary History of the Junior and Community College Movement*. New York: Greenwood Press.

Dewey, J. (1916). *Democracy and Education*. New York: MacMillan Company.

Dewey, J. (1956). *Philosophy of Education*. Ames, IA: Littlefield, Adams, and Co.

Diekhoff, J. (1950). *Democracy's College: Higher Education in the Local Community*. New York: Harper and Brothers.

Dimaggio, P. and Powell, W. (1983). The Iron Cage Revisited: Institutional Isomorphism and Collective Rationality in Organizational Fields. *American Sociological Review, 48*(2), 147-160.

Dougherty, K. (1994). *The Contradictory College: The Conflicting Origins, Impacts, and Futures of the Community College*. Albany: State University of New York Press.

Dougherty, K. and Bakia, M. (2000). Community Colleges and Contract Training: Content, Origins, and Impact. *Teachers College Record, 102*(1), 197-243.

Dowd, A. (2003). From Access to Outcome Equity: Revitalizing the Democratic Mission of the Community College. *The Annals of the American Academy of Political and Social Science,* (586), 92-119.

Drury, R. (2001). The Entrepreneurial Community College: Bringing Workforce, Economic and Community Development to Virginia Communities. *Inquiry Magazine, 6*(1), 1-10.

Duffy, R. (2005). Political Mobilization, Venue Change, and Coal-Bed Methane Conflict. *Natural Resources Journal, 45*(2), 409-440.

Eaton, J. (2005). Why Community Colleges Shouldn't Offer Baccalaureates. *The Chronicle of Higher Education, 52*(10), B25-26.

Edmundson, M. (2004). *Why read?* New York: Bloomsbury.

Elshtain, J. (1993). *Democracy on Trial*. New York: Basic Books.

Engel, M. (2000). *The Struggle for Control in Public Education: Market Ideology vs. Democratic Values*. Philadelphia: Temple University Press.

Etzioni, A. (2001). *Next: The Road to the Good Society*. New York: Basic Books.

Farnsworth, K. (2001). The Values of a Global Perspective. *Community College Journal, 71*(4), 8-14.

Farnsworth, K. (2006). The Four Lessons that Community Colleges can Learn from For-Profit Institutions. *The Chronicle of Higher Education, 53*(10), B17-18.

Floyd, D., M. Skolnik and K. Walker Eds. (2005). *The Community College Baccalaureate: Emerging Trends and Policy Issues*. Sterling, VA: Stylus.

Flynn, W. (1999). Rethinking Teaching and Learning. *Community College Journal, 70*(4). 8-13

Frisch, M. (1991). *Alexander Hamilton and the Political Order: An Interpretation of His Political Thought and Practice.* Lanham, Maryland: University Press of America.

Frye, J. (1994). Educational Paradigms in the Professional Literature of the Community College. Pp. 181-224 in *The Higher Education Handbook of Theory and Research.* New York: Agathon.

Gallagher, E. (1994). *Jordan and Lange: The California Junior College as Protector of Teaching.* Palo Alto, CA: Hoover Institution on War, Revolution and Peace; Stanford University.

Gamson, Z. (1997). Higher Education and Rebuilding Civic Life. *Change, 29*(1), 10-13.

Gedicks, A. (1993). *The New Resource Wars: Native and Environmental Struggles Against Multinational Corporations.* Boston: South End press.

Gleazer, E. (1969). *This is the Community College.* Boston: Houghton-Mifflin.

Gleazer, E. (1981). *The Community College: Values, Vision, Vitality.* Washington, D.C.: American Association of Community and Junior Colleges.

Goodwin, G. (1973). *A Social Panacea: A History of the Community-Junior College Ideology.* Washington, D.C.: U.S. Department of Health, Education, and Welfare.

Goyette, K. and Mullen, A. (2006). Who Studies the Arts and Sciences? Social Background and the Choice and Consequences of Undergraduate Field of Study. *The Journal of Higher Education, 77*(3), 497-638.

Grant, G. (1979). Implications of Competence-Based Education. Pp. 1-17 in *On Competence: A Critical Analysis of Competence-Based Reforms in Higher Education.* Edited by G. Grant. San Francisco: Jossey-Bass.

Greenwood, R., Suddaby, R., and Hinings, C.R. (2002). Theorizing Change: The Role of Professional Associations in the Transformation of Institutionalized Fields. *Academy of Management Journal, 45*(1), 58-80.

Griffith, M. and Connor, A. (1994). *Democracy's Open Door: The Community College in America's Future.* Portsmouth, NH: Boynton-Cook Publishers.

Grubb, N. (1996). The New Vocationalism: What it is, What it could be. *Phi Delta Kappan, 77*(8), 535-546.

Hanson, C. (1998). From Teaching to Learning: Are We Still Educating Students? *The Teaching Professor, 12*(8), 1.

Hanson, C. (2000). Silence and Structure in the Classroom: From Seminar to Town Meeting Via Post-Its. *The National Teaching and Learning Forum, 9*(6), 1-4.

Hanson, C. (2003). The Promise of Democracy's College: Town Hall Meeting as Teaching Method. *The Community College Journal of Research and Practice, 27*(3), 173-90.

Harper, W. R. (1968). Changes Affecting the Small College Which may be Expected and Which are to be Desired. Pp. 53-59 in *Growth of An American Invention: A Documentary History of the Community College Movement.* Edited by T. Diener. New York: Greenwood Press.

Hersh, R. and Merrow, J. (Eds). (2005). *Declining By Degrees: Higher Education at Risk*. New York: Palgrave.

Higginbottom, G. and Romano, R. (2001). SUNY General Education Reform and the Community Colleges: A Case Study of Cross-Purposes. Pp. 243-259 in *Community Colleges: Policy in the Future Context*. Edited by B. Townsend and S. Twombly. Westport, CT: Ablex Publishing.

Honig, M. (2004). "The New Middle Management: Intermediary Organizations in Education Policy Implementation." *Educational Evaluation and Policy Analysis, 26*(1), 65-87.

Jackson, P. (1968). *Life in Classrooms*. New York: Holt, Rhinehart and Winston.

Jacobs, J. and Dougherty, K. (2006). The Uncertain Future of the Community College Workforce Development Mission. Pp. 53-62 in "Community College Mission in the 21st Century." Edited by B. Townsend and K. Dougherty. *New Directions for Community Colleges*, no. 136.

Jordan, D. S. (1910). The Care and Culture of Freshman. *North American Review* CXCI, April, 441-42.

Karabel, J. (1972). Community Colleges and Social Stratification. *Harvard Educational Review, 42*(4), 521-61.

Kellog, A. (2001). Looking Inward, Freshman Care Less About Politics and More About Money. *Chronicle of Higher Education, 48*(3), A47.

Kelly, A. and Harbison, W. (1970). *The American Constitution: Its Origins and Development* (Fourth Edition). New York: W.W. Norton.

Knefelkamp, L. and Schneider, C. (1997). Education for a World Lived in Common with Others. Pp. 321-344 in *Education and Democracy: Re-imagining Liberal Learning in America*. Edited by R. Orrill. New York: The College Board.

Knowles, M. (1973). *The Adult Learner: A Neglected Species*. Houston, Gulf Publications.

Labaree, D. (1997). *How to Succeed in School...Without Really Learning*. New Haven: Yale University Press.

Labaree, D. (1997). Public Goods, Private Goods: The American Struggle Over Educational Goals. *American Educational Research Journal, 34*(1), 39-81.

Lasch, C. (1995). *The Revolt of the Elites and the Betrayal of Democracy*. New York: W.W. Norton.

Lavelle, M. (2001). High Stakes on the Prairie. *U.S. News and World Report*. March 12, 52-54.

Lazerson, M., Wagener, U. and Shumanis, N. (2000). What Makes a Revolution? Teaching and Learning in Higher Education 1980-2000. *Change, 32*(3), 12-19.

Leonard, G. (1992). The End of School. *The Atlantic Monthly, 140*(5), 24-27.

Levin, J. (2000). The Revised Institution: The Community College Mission at the End of the Twentieth Century. *Community College Review, 28*(2), 1-25.

Levin, J. (2001). *Globalizing the Community College: Strategies for Change in the 21st Century*. New York: Palgrave.

Levin, J. (2002). Global Culture and the Community College. *Community College Journal of Research and Practice, (26)*2, 121-145.

Levin, J. (2004). The Community College as a Baccalaureate Granting Institution. *The Review of Higher Education, 28*(1), 1-22.

Lopez Pintor, R., Gratschew, M., and Sullivan, K. (2007). *Voter Turnout Rates from a Comparative Perspective*. Retrieved January 23, 2007, from www.idea.int/ publications/vt/upload/voter%20turnout.pdf.

Lyall, K., and Sell, K. (2006). *The True Genius of America at Risk*. Westport, CT: Praeger.

Macionis, J. (2007). *Sociology* 11th Edition. Upper Saddle River, NJ: Prentice-Hall.

Mager, R. (1975). *Preparing Instructional Objectives*. Belmont, CA: Fearon-Pitman.

Marks, H. (1990). *The College Experience: Differential Gender Effects on the Development of Social Responsibility*. Paper Presented at the American Educational Research Association. Boston, MA.

McCall, G. and Simmons, J. (1966). *Identities and Interactions*. New York: The Free Press.

McGrath, D. and Spear, M. (1991). *The Academic Crisis of the Community College*. Albany, NY: State University of New York Press.

McKee, J. (2005). Westark's Workforce Baccalaureate. Pp. 129-138 in *The Community College Baccalaureate: Emerging Trends and Policy Issues*. Edited by D. Floyd, M. Skolnick, and K. Walker. Sterling, VA: Stylus.

Mead, G. H. (1934). *Mind, Self, and Society*. Chicago: University of Chicago Press.

Medsker, L. (1960). *The Junior College: Progress and Prospect*. New York: McGraw-Hill.

Merisotis, J. and Phipps, R. (1999). What's the Difference? *Change, 31*(3), 12-17.

Metcalf, A. (2005). Towards a Theory of Intermediating Organizations: Agency Between Academy, Industry, and Government. Paper Presented at the annual Triple Helix conference, Turin Italy. May, 2005.

Mills, K. (2003). Community College Baccalaureates: Some Critics Decry the Trend as Mission Creep. National Cross Talk. Published by the National Center for Public Policy and Higher Education. www.highereducation.org /crosstalk/ct0103/news0103-community.html.

Moriarty, D. (1996). The Past is Prologue. *Community College Journal, 67(*2), 3-4.

Newman, F., Couturier, L. and Scurry, J. (2004). *The Future of Higher Education: Rhetoric, Reality, and the Risks of the Market*. San Fransciso: Jossey-Bass.

Norton, R. (1997). *DACUM Handbook*. Columbus, OH: Center on Education and Training for Employment.

O'Banion, T. (1997a). *A Learning College for the 21ˢᵗ Century*. Phoenix: Oryx Press.

O'Banion, T. (1997b). The Learning Revolution: A Guide for Community College Trustees. *Trustee Quarterly, 1*(1), 2-19.

O'Banion, T. (1997c). *Creating More Learning-Centered Community Colleges*. Mission Viejo, CA: League for Innovation in the Community College and Peoplesoft, Inc.

O'Banion, T. (1998a). The Learning Revolution: Perched at the Millennium. *Community College Week, 10*(12), 12-15.

O'Banion, T. (1998b). The Center of the Learning Revolution. *Community College Week, 10*(4), 24-26.

Orr, D. (1994). *Earth in Mind: On Education, Environment, and the Human Prospect*. Washington, D.C.: Island Press.

Ozga, J. and Lawn, M. (1988). Schoolwork: Interpreting the Labor Process of Teaching, *British Journal of Sociology of Education, 9*(3), 323-36.

Parks Dolaz, L., Keen, C., Keen, J. and Dolaz Parks, S. (1996). Lives of Commitment: Higher Education in the Life of the New Commons. *Change, 28*(3), 11-15.

Parrington, V. L. (1927). *Main Currents in American Thought*. New York: Harcourt, Brace and World Inc.

Pascarella, E. and Terenzini, P. (1991). *How College Affects Students*. San Francisco: Jossey-Bass.

Pascarella, E. and Terenzini, P. (2005). *How College Affects Students: A Third Decade of Research*. San Francisco: Jossey-Bass.

Perelman, L. (1992). *Schools Out—A Radical New Formula for the Revitalization of Americas Educational System*. New York: Avon Books.

Perkins, J. (2004). *Confessions of an Economic Hit Man*. San Francisco: Berret-Koehler Publishers.

Pfeffer, J. and Salancik, G. (1978). *The External Control of Organizations*. New York: Harper and Row.

Pickelman, J. (2005). NHMCCD: A Community Partner with Entrepreneurial Spirit. Pp. 23-35 in *The Entrepreneurial Community College*. Edited by J. Roueche and B. Jones. Washington, D.C.: Community College Press.

Pincus, F. (1980). The False Promise of the Community Colleges: Class Conflict and Vocational Education. *Harvard Educational Review, 50*(3), 332-361.

Putnam, R. (2000). *Bowling Alone: The Collapse and Revival of American Community*. New York: Simon and Schuster.

Ramage, J. and Bean, J. (1989). *Writing Arguments*. New York: Macmillan.

Rhoades, G. (1998). *Managed Professionals: Unionized Faculty and Restructuring Academic Labor*. Albany, NY, State University of New York Press.

Rhoads, R. and Valadez, J. (1996). *Democracy, Multiculturalism, and the Community College*. New York: Garland.

Rice, E. (2004). The Future of the American Faculty: An Interview with Martin J. Finkelstein and Jack H. Schuster, *Change, 36*(2), 26-35.

Roksa, J. (2006). Does the Vocational Focus of Community Colleges Hinder Student's Educational Attainment? *The Review of Higher Education, 29*(4), 499-526.

Romano, R. (2003). Financing Community Colleges Across the States: An Economic Perspective. Presented at the Cornell Higher Education Research Institute (CHERI) conference "The Complex Community College," October 13-14, 2003. Ithaca, NY.

Romano, R. (Ed.). (2002). *Internationalizing the Community College.* Washington, D.C.: The Community College Press.

Rouche, J. and Jones, B. (Eds.). (2005). *The Entrepreneurial Community College.* Washington, D.C.: Community College Press.

Sanford, N. (1962). *The American College.* New York: Wiley.

Sax, L., Astin, A., Korn, W. and Mahoney, K. (1999). *The American Freshman: National Norms for Fall 1999.* Los Angeles: Higher Education Research Institute, UCLA.

Sax, L., Astin, A., Korn, W. and Mahoney, K. (2000). *The American Freshman: National Norms for Fall 2000.* Los Angeles: Higher Education Research Institute, UCLA.

Sax, L., Astin, A., Lindholm, J., Korn, S., Saenz, V. and Mahoney, K. (2003). *The American Freshman: National Norms for Fall 2003.* Los Angeles: Higher Education Research Institute, UCLA.

Sax, L., Astin, A., Lindholm, J., Korn, S., Saenz, V. and Mahoney, K. (2007). *The American Freshman: National Norms for Fall 2007.* Los Angeles: Higher Education Research Institute, UCLA.

Schneider, C. (2005). Liberal Education: Slip-Sliding Away? Pp. 61-76 in *Declining By Degrees: Higher Education at Risk.* Edited by R. Hersh and J. Merrow. New York: Palgrave.

Schultz, D. (2005). The Corporate University in American Society. *Logos: A journal of Modern Society and Culture.* www.logosjournal.com/issue_4.4/schultz.htm

Schuyler, G. (1999). A Historical and Contemporary View of the Community College Curriculum. Pp. 31-15 in Trends in Community College Curriculum. Edited by G. Schuyler, *New Directions for Community Colleges*, No. 108. San Francisco: Jossey-Bass.

Selingo, J. (2004). U.S. Public's Confidence in Colleges Remains High. *The Chronicle of Higher Education, 50*(35), 1,10.

Shapiro, H. (2005). *A Larger Sense of Purpose: Higher Education and Society.* Princeton, NJ: Princeton University Press.

Shaw, K. and Jacobs, J. (2003). Community Colleges: New Environments, New Directions. *The Annals of the American Academy of Political and Social Science,* (586), 6-15.

Shor, I. (1980). *Critical Teaching and Everyday Life.* Chicago: University of Chicago Press.

Skinner, B. F. (1964). New Methods and New Aims in Teaching. *New Scientist 122*(5), 483-484.

Soine, R. (2003). A Framework for Learning Design, *Techniques, 78*(3), 38-41.

Stalloff, D. (2005). *Hamilton, Adams, Jefferson: The Politics of Enlightenment and the American Founding.* New York: Hill and Wang.

Stiglitz, J. (2002). *Globalization and its Discontents.* New York: W.W. Norton.

Sullivan, W. M. (1997). *The University as Citizen: Institutional Identity and Social Responsibility.* Washington, D.C.: Council of Public Policy Education.

Taylor, F. W. (1967). *The Practice of Scientific Management.* New York, W.W. Norton.

Thatcher, M. (1987). AIDS Education, and the Year 2000. *Woman's Own Magazine, 55*(10), 10.

Tierney, W. (1991). Ideology and Identity in Postsecondary Institutions. Pp. 35-57 in *Culture and Ideology in Higher Education: Advancing a Critical Agenda* edited by W. Tierney. New York: Praeger.

Tow, K. (2001). The Global Student. *Community College Journal, 71*(4), 30-31.

Townsend, B. (2005). A Cautionary View. Pp. 179-190 in *The Community College Baccalaureate: Emerging Trends and Policy Issues.* Edited by D. Floyd, M. Skolnick, and K. Walker. Sterling, VA: Stylus.

U.S. Department of Education. (2004). *The 21st Century Community College: A Strategic Guide to Maximizing Labor Market Responsiveness.* Washington, D.C.: U.S. Department of Education.

Veblen, T. (1957). *The Higher Learning in America: a Memorandum on the Conduct of Universities by Business Men.* New York, Hill and Wang.

Vidal, G. (1983). On Rereading the Oz Books. Pp. 256-270 in *The Wizard of Oz: The Critical Heritage Series*, Edited by M. P. Hearn. New York: Shocken Books.

Walker, K. and Floyd, D. (2005). Applied and Workforce Baccalaureates. Pp. 95-102 in *The Community College Baccalaureate: Emerging Trends and Policy Issues.* Edited by D. Floyd, M. Skolnick, and K. Walker. Sterling, VA: Stylus.

Wattenbarger, J. (2000). Colleges Should Stick to What They do Best. *Communty College Week, 12*(18), 4-5.

Willimon, W. and Naylor, T. (1995). *The Abandoned Generation: Rethinking Higher Education.* Grand Rapids, MI: William B. Eerdmans.

Wingspread Group on Higher Education. (1993). *An American Imperative: Higher Expectations for Higher Education.* Racine, WI: The Johnson Foundation Inc.

Wolf, A. (2002). *Does Education Matter? Myths about Education and Economic Growth.* London: Penguin Books.

Worldwide Instruction Design System (WIDS) (web site) http://www.wids. org/ index.php?option=com_content&task=blogsection&id=7&Itemid=29 (accessed 21 April 2006).

Worldwide Instruction Design System (WIDS) (web site) http://www.wids.org/ index.php?option=com_content&task=view&id=17&Itemid=64 (accessed 4 May 2006).

Worldwide Instruction Design System (WIDS) (web site) www.wids.org (accessed 14 May 2007).

Zemsky, R., Wegner, G and Massey, W. (2005). Today's Colleges Must be Market Smart and Mission Centered. *The Chronicle of Higher Education, 52*(45), B6-B7.

Zwerling, S. (1976). *Second Best: The Crisis of the Community College.* New York: McGraw-Hill.

Index